EASTERN ORTHODOXY: A WAY OF LIFE

By the Rev. Anthony M. Coniaris

Z
F O S
E

LIGHT AND LIFE PUBLISHING COMPANY
Minneapolis, Minnesota

Printed in the United States of America

INTRODUCTION

WHILE ORTHODOXY HAS, among its varied store of treasures, a magnificent tradition of preaching, it would be fanciful to suggest that that tradition has been renewed and maintained in all its greatness in modern times. It would be equally wrong to suppose that pulpit standards of the Old World, even if high, can apply in our contemporary situation.

As the forms and norms—indeed even the language—of traditional preaching have become increasingly difficult to bend to the changing needs of Orthodoxy in America, two things have happened. The pulpit has come to enjoy a new import-ance in our churches; and it has often been the setting for a fresh and stimulating approach to the high ministry of preach-ing.

The volume in hand stands in this new "tradition," and I am pleased to commend it to the reader. Rich in apt illustra-tion, its chapters tightly yet gracefully written, it ranges with a pastor's perception and compassion over a broad spectrum of human issues. In short, it validates its title, for it addresses itself wisely yet unassumingly to the ordinary man of faith looking for "a way of life." I pray it will be an instrument of God's grace wherever it goes.

Archbishop IAKOVOS
Archbishop of the Greek Orthodox
Church in North and South America

CONTENTS

Chapter One

THE MEANING OF LIFE

RECENTLY A HUGE JET AIRLINER experienced electrical failure and lost contact with the airport. It wandered about in the fog for three hours. When the passengers learned they were out of contact with the steady signals which guided the huge ship, they were terrified. It was a real nightmare.

No less a nightmare are the lives of many people today who wander through life aimlessly with no purpose, no destination, no goal.

A certain author writes: "The greatest misery of man is neither poverty nor sickness nor misfortune in life, nor the disappointments of the heart nor death; it is the misery of not knowing why he is born, suffers and dies."

What is the meaning of life? How am I to get rhyme or reason out of the life I am now living? I wake, I eat, I work, I sleep, I repeat the same process day after day and year after year. But why? For what purpose? Just to wear out and be discarded like a suit of old clothes? Just to move on and make room for others? How am I to fit all the puzzling pieces of my life into a sensible and purposeful pattern— my unemployment, my hospital bills, my bitter disappointments, my failures, my heartaches? Why must these things be? Is there an intelligent plan that lies behind them all; a plan that gives meaning to life?

A noted Swiss psychiatrist writes, "Man can bear great physical or spiritual hardships, *but what he cannot bear is the sense of meaninglessness*. We must find some way in which our lives count, in which they seem important, or we go mad."

Dr. Viktor Frankl, the Viennese psychiatrist who spent time in a Nazi concentration camp during the last war, reports that those who survived the atrocities of the concentration camps were those who had a goal, those for whom life had meaning. Those for whom life held no meaning gave up and died.

What is the meaning of life? Consider some of the answers that have been given to this question.

Sartre, the French existentialist, writes, "I thought vaguely of doing away with myself, to do away with at least one of these superfluous existences. But my death, my corpse, my blood, poured out on this gravel, among these plants, in this smiling garden would have been superfluous as well. I was superfluous to all eternity." * It makes no difference whether one be dead or alive—life is superfluous, meaningless, says Sartre.

Other existentialists tell us that life is a plague, that there is no permanent self, no direction or destiny. The self is poised over nothingness. Man has no name, no passport; he is like a letter without an address. They describe life in terms such as "dread," "nausea," and "the death motif." All is despair and loneliness. And this theme seems to have penetrated every aspect of life today.

After hearing all this we can understand how the Apostle Paul must have felt when he asked: "Wretched man that I am! Who shall deliver me from the body of this death?" We too might well ask: Wretched man that I am, who shall deliver me from all this meaninglessness, from this "dread" and "nausea" of life, from this loneliness and despair? The answer St. Paul gave to his question applies to ours: "I thank God through Jesus Christ our Lord" (Rom. 7:24, 25). It is God through Christ who can deliver us from a meaningless existence to a purposeful life.

Someone has said that modern man is like a page torn from the middle of a book. It has no relationship to what went before and none to what comes after. Hence, it has no meaning. Man needs a connectedness with the past and with the future. He needs a sense of belonging to the Great Eternal—God. It is this sense of belonging to God that we find in Christ who died for us because we belong to Him and are infinitely precious to Him. It is in this act of love on Calvary that life finds its greatest meaning.

Halford Luccock tells of the woman who went to the

---

* Sartre, "Boulevard Noir," quoted in Marcel's *Philosophy of Existence.*

top of the Empire State Building, one hundred and two
stories high. She looked down on the sidewalks, and the people were so far away that they looked like ants. She said, "I
imagine this is the way people look to God." There is no doubt
that much of the meaninglessness of life today can be traced
to the fact that people feel that they are like ants in the eyes
of God—insignificant, forgotten, uncared for, unloved, unnoticed.

But if we wish to know exactly how people look to God
we must climb not the Empire State Building but a hill called
Calvary and look at a man on a cross. There in the light of
that cross we see how people look to God: "God so loved the
world that he gave his only Son that whoever believes in him
should not perish but have eternal life." That is how people
appear to God! That is where we find meaning for life.

"But while he [the Prodigal Son] was yet at a distance,
his father saw him and had compassion, and ran and embraced
him and kissed him. And the son said to him, 'Father, I have
sinned against heaven and before you; I am no longer worthy
to be called your son! But the father said to his servants,
'Bring quickly the best robe, and put it on him, and put a
ring on his hand and shoes on his feet; and bring the fatted
calf and kill it, and let us eat and make merry; for this my
son was dead and is alive again; he was lost, and is found"
(Luke 15:20–24). "I say to you," said Jesus, "that likewise
joy shall be in heaven over one sinner who repents." Here is
meaning for life!

Life is a plague, say the existentialists. Jesus says, "I am
the light of the world; he who follows me shall not walk in
darkness but shall have the light of life" (John 8:12).

Life is nausea, say those who deny God. Jesus says, "I am
the bread of life; he who comes to me shall never hunger;
and he who believes in me shall never thirst" (John 6:35).

Life is dread, some people maintain. Jesus says, "I came
that they may have life and have it abundantly."

But, you ask, how can you say there is meaning in life
when there is so much evil and suffering? so much distress
and anguish? Look at the cross again. It was willed by wicked
men, but God wove it into the salvation of the world. The

greatest good came from the greatest evil. Our thorns, too, can become a crown if we live lives that are surrendered to Christ. "With them that love Him God cooperates in *all* things for good," says St. Paul. And he goes on: "For this slight momentary affliction is preparing for us an eternal weight of glory beyond all comparison" (II Cor. 4:17). Here is meaning for life even in suffering!

All well and good, says another, but how can life have any meaning at all in the face of death? Have you ever stood in a cemetery watching a loved one being lowered into an open grave? What possible meaning can life have in the face of that? It would have no meaning at all, if it were not for One who came back from the grave and proclaimed triumphantly, "I am the resurrection and the life; he who believes in Me, though he were dead, yet shall he live, and he who lives and believes in Me shall have life everlasting." Here is meaning for life especially in the face of death!

Life without a goal is like a ship on the high seas without a port, without a destination. It just keeps sailing and sailing knowing that there is no harbor, no haven, no goal, no reunion, no arriving. How monotonous such a voyage would be! How dreadfully dull! No wonder existentialists who deny God speak of life in terms of "plague" "dread," and "nausea."

Contrast this with St. Paul whose purpose and goal in life was Christ: "For me to live is Christ," he said. Christ gave so much meaning to his life that he could say: "Eye has not seen; ear has not heard, nor has it ever entered into the heart of man, what things God has prepared for those who love him." Toward the end of his life he could say, "I have fought the good fight. I have finished the race. I have kept the faith. Henceforth, there is laid up for me the crown of righteousness, which the Lord, the righteous judge, will award to me on that Day, and not only to me but also to all who have loved his appearing" (II Tim. 4:8).

Here is meaning for life! Meaning that comes to those who accept this Jesus as Lord and follow Him as Master; those who commit their lives to Him and lose themselves in service to others; those who live in close communion with Him through daily prayer, regular reading of His Word, and faithful participation in church worship and the Sacraments.

The airliner that was lost in the fog eventually re-established contact with the airport and was guided in for a safe landing. If we are to find our way out of the fog of meaninglessness that surrounds us today, we, too, must establish a living, personal relationship with Him who is "the way, the truth and the life," who alone can lead us to the abundant life full of purpose and meaning both for now and for all eternity.

Chapter Two

WHAT IS YOUR GOAL IN LIFE?

A TRAVELER PASSING THROUGH a small town asked an old man: "What is this place noted for?"

"Mister," replied the old man, "this is the starting point for any place in the world. You can start here and go anywhere you wish."

Youth is such a starting point. One can start from youth to go almost anywhere he desires.

Where one goes in life depends to a large extent on the destination one chooses, the goal one selects.

At no other period of life does a person make so many important decisions as he does in youth. It is in his youth that he chooses his vocation, his marriage partner, and his goal for life. And almost every decision he makes—whether it be a vocation or a marriage partner—will depend on the goal he has chosen for himself.

A person asked one day: "How is it that one sailboat goes one way, another the opposite way while the wind blows over the lake in only one direction?"

An old sailor replied, "It's the set of the sails that makes the difference."

So it is with us. The winds of life beat upon us, but the direction we take in life depends upon the set of our sails, on the goal we have chosen.

To choose a goal is to give purpose and meaning to life. A little girl asked her mother one day, "Mommy, how can you stand to wash dishes day in and day out without ever seeming to get really fed up with it?" The mother answered the question with perfect honesty: "Honey," she said. "I'm not just washing dishes; I'm building a home." She had a goal that gave meaning and purpose even to dishwashing.

To choose a goal brings power to life. Many years ago Notre Dame was losing a football game. It was hopelessly outclassed by the opposing team. During half time a young woman burst into the locker room and with tears in her eyes said, "Men, you must win this game for my dying brother. He is an alumnus of this school, and is listening. He will be gone in a few days, but will die content if the game is won. You must win for him." When they went onto the field for the second half they were a different team. They were the same players but they were fired by a new inspiration. They won the game, not because of their outstanding ability, but because they had an inspiring sense of purpose, a great goal!

Yet youth today hesitates to choose a goal. "Life is so uncertain," they say, "that I cannot set a goal. How can anyone make plans in a world like ours, in a world where any minute the Bomb may be dropped?"

No matter how uncertain life may be—and it has always been uncertain—we must choose a goal, otherwise we will drift and flounder.

Why all the over-emphasis on sex today? Is it not an indication that our civilization is drifting, that it has no really worthwhile purpose or goal? Sex falls into its natural God-given place only when man knows what life is for. If man does not know why he is living, then sex is degraded from its lofty intention to serve as mere diversion for people who are frustrated by the cheap character of the life surrounding them. Recently, an article appeared in some newspapers entitled, "Sex in Scandinavia." The article concluded with these words: "But what above all marks the Scandinavians' attitude toward sex is their refusal to pretend, even in polite society, that it does not exist." It is not that we are refusing today to pretend that sex does not exist. It is that we have gone to the other extreme. It is that we have lost our bearings and are pretending that *it is the only thing that exists*. This happens when we lose sight of the real meaning of life.

Why is it that most people today follow the crowd? Why is there so much "keeping up with the Joneses"? Is it not because people refuse to choose their own goal in life; they refuse to direct their own lives; they prefer to let the crowd run their lives? A person who chooses his own goal in life is never a thermometer personality—reflecting his environment—but always a thermostat personality—influencing and changing his environment.

Many people today are saying that life is not worthwhile. What they are really saying is that they themselves have no personal goals which are worthwhile. Without a goal we may have plenty to live on, but we have nothing to live for. A pastor once asked a college student, "What are you living for?" The student answered, "I am going to be a pharmacist." The pastor said, "I understand that this is how you are going to earn your livelihood, but what are you *living* for?"

What are we living for?

An animal does not have to choose a goal. It comes into the world with a built-in goal that is pre-set and limited to two things: self-preservation and procreation. Of all beings in this world only man has been created by God with the power to choose and formulate his own goal. Of course, this makes it much more difficult for man. It means that he must distinguish between worthy and unworthy goals and choose the one which he feels is most worthy.

An animal cannot fail to fulfill its destiny; but you and I can. As the German author Thielicke says, "We can play the wrong role. We can choose the wrong goal. We can climb the wrong mountain and reach the wrong summit. And at the Last Judgment there may be written on the margin of our life in red ink: 'You missed the whole point.' "

What is life's most worthy goal?

Carlyle said once, "I have no objection, even as a Christian, to your deriving man from previous animal forms and declaring that the monkey is his grandfather and the tadpole his great-grandfather. Why should I? This is something for science to inquire into.

"But I have objections to something else. I object to your saying that therefore the nature of man, that your nature and my nature is like that of a tadpole. No, if you are going to define the mystery of man, if you are going to define what God has in mind for man and what he breathed into him, then you cannot say, 'He is only a little more than a tadpole.' Then you must say, 'He is little less than God.' In other words, you cannot define man on the basis of his biological origin; you must define him in the light of his destiny, his goal.

"Actually, you must enter upon another level. The mystery of man can be understood only if you put him into relation to Him who gives him his life, who calls him by his name, sacrifices His most beloved for him on Calvary, and never rests until He has drubbed him out of his alienation, his madness, his fear, and his guilt and brought him back home to His peace."

Man's true and greatest goal in life is God, Christ. It was this goal man was made to serve. "Thou shalt love the Lord thy God with all thy heart and with all thy mind and with all thy strength and with all thy soul." Perfect Truth and Perfect Good are to be found only in God. Complete fulfillment is impossible except in Him. The man who has Christ as a goal knows a peace and happiness such as the world cannot give and cannot destroy. The man who has Christ as a goal will not complain that life is not worth living; life will always have meaning and it will have power. The man who has Christ as a goal starts on a journey that will lead him on into eternity and the glorious presence of God.

The pioneers who climbed Mt. Everest waged a tremendous battle to reach the summit. Yet they tell us that so long as they could see the peak, no matter how far in the distance, they had the inspiration to keep climbing.

So it is with us. If we keep our eyes on Christ, our goal, and continue to press toward the mark of His high calling, His light will shine through the gloom. In every storm He will be our shelter. In every weakness He will be our strength. In every hunger He will be the bread of life. And in death He will be our life.

Chapter Three

THE JESUS PRAYER

"As Jesus drew near to Jericho a blind man was sitting by the roadside begging. . . ."

To CATCH THE TRUE MEANING of these words, one must remember that the "roadside" by which the blind man was sitting was the gutter of some street in Jericho. He was blind, and he was a beggar sitting in the gutter. To the people of Jericho he was the lowest of the low.

". . . and hearing a multitude going by, he inquired what this meant. They told him, 'Jesus of Nazareth is passing by.' And he cried, 'Jesus, Son of David, have mercy on me!' And those who were in front rebuked him telling him to be silent."

He knew of Jesus. He believed in Him. He cried out to Him with faith. But those around him rebuked him, "Quiet! The Master is busy! He's teaching a crowd of people. Do you think He would pay attention to you, a dirty, blind beggar wallowing in the gutter? How dare you trouble the Master; you—a nobody; you—the lowest of the low; you—the scum of the earth!"

". . . but he cried out all the more, 'Son of David, have mercy on me!' "

He didn't give up. No obstacles, no discouragements could stop him. He had heard what Jesus could do and had done. And nothing was going to stop him from making contact with Jesus. He cried out even louder than before, "Son of David, have mercy on me!"

"And Jesus stopped."

Above all the noise of the multitude Jesus heard the lonely prayer of the blind beggar and *He stopped*. The Almighty

Lord and Master of the universe is stopped by the prayer of
a poor, blind forgotten beggar sitting in the gutter—a nobody!
He commands the beggar to be brought to Him.

" '*What do you want me to do for you?' He asks. 'Lord,
let me receive my sight.' And Jesus said to him, 'Receive your
sight; your faith has made you well.' And immediately he received his sight and followed him, glorifying God; and all
the people, when they saw it, gave praise to God.*"

Let us talk briefly about the prayer that stopped Jesus:
"Jesus, Son of David, have mercy on me." For certainly if
this prayer stopped Jesus then, it can stop Him today.

The blind man's prayer, altered but slightly, is known today as the Jesus prayer: "Lord Jesus Christ, Son of God, have
mercy on me, a sinner." It is one of the most commonly used
prayers in the Eastern Orthodox Church. We read about it in
that classic of Russian Orthodoxy, *The Way of a Pilgrim*. This
book is the story of an unnamed peasant who seeks out someone
who will teach him how to fulfill the Biblical command to
"pray without ceasing."

He wanders through Russia and Siberia with a knapsack
of dried bread for food and the charity of men for shelter. He
asks many church authorities and religious people, but none
can teach him how to pray without ceasing. He is about to
come away from his journey empty-hearted when at last he
meets a holy man who teaches him the Jesus prayer: "Lord
Jesus. . . ." From this man he learns that to pray without ceasing is "a constant, uninterrupted calling upon the divine name
of Jesus during every occupation, at all times, at all places,
even during sleep." He learns to repeat it as many as 12,000
times a day without effort. The Jesus prayer becomes a constant, warming presence within him, and brings him great
joy.

What is so different about the Jesus prayer?

Prayer, to the average man, is asking God for something.
The Jesus prayer is not this. It is an attempt—a scientific
attempt—to change the one who prays.

St. John Chrysostom tells us how this can happen:

"I implore you, brethren, never to break or despise the

rule of this prayer: A Christian when he eats, drinks, walks, sits, travels or does any other thing must continually cry: 'Lord Jesus Christ, Son of God, have mercy upon me.' So that the name of the Lord Jesus descending into the depths of the heart, should subdue the serpent ruling over the inner pastures and bring life and salvation to the soul. He should always live with the name of the Lord Jesus, so that the heart swallows the Lord and the Lord the heart, and the two become one. And again: do not estrange your heart from God, but abide in Him, and always guard your heart by remembering our Lord Jesus Christ, until the name of the Lord becomes rooted in the heart and it ceases to think anything else."

Another Father of the Church says: "Continue constantly in the name of the Lord Jesus that the heart may swallow the Lord and the Lord the heart, and that these two may be one. However, this is not accomplished in a single day, nor in two days, but requires many years and much time."

There is tremendous power in the name of Jesus. St. Paul says: *"Everyone who calls upon the name of the Lord will be saved"* (Rom. 10:13). *"Christ Jesus . . . humbled himself and became obedient to death, even death on a cross. Therefore God has highly exalted him and given him the name that is above every name, that in the name of Jesus every knee should bow, of things in heaven, and things on earth and things under the earth"* (Phil. 2:5–10). Jesus says in John 14:13, *"If you ask anything in my name, I will do it."* St Peter says, *"And there is salvation in no one else, for there is no other name under heaven given among men by which we must be saved"* (Acts 4:12). The power of the Jesus prayer, then, lies in the name Jesus, "the name that is above every name." Thus, the name "Jesus" alone can fulfill the whole need of the one who prays when it is prayed with faith and with a life that is lived in obedience to Christ. For, as our Lord said, "Not everyone who *says* to me, 'Lord, Lord,' shall enter the kingdom of heaven but he who *does* the will of my father who is in heaven" (Matt. 7:21).

Many times we wonder how the early Christian martyrs marched to their death so courageously. We cease to wonder about the source of their courage, however, when we consider the life of St. Ignatius, the God-bearer, Bishop of Antioch, who was crowned in Rome with a martyr's death under the emperor Trajan. We read about him: "When they were taking him to be devoured by wild beasts and he had the name of Jesus constantly on his lips, the pagans asked him why he unceasingly remembered that name. The saint replied that he had the name of Jesus Christ written in his heart and that he confessed with his mouth Him whom he always carried in his heart." The Jesus prayer gave him the power to face death victoriously.

The Jesus prayer can give us the same power to resist every evil thought and temptation with which Satan attacks us. For example, when Satan knocks on the door of the mind seeking entrance through some evil thought, send Jesus to the door and he will flee. Resist every temptation with the Jesus prayer. As soon as you feel that the stronghold of your soul is being assaulted by Satan, start praying the Jesus prayer constantly and with faith. Satan will flee. St. John Climacus says, "With the name of Jesus flog the foes, because there is no stronger weapon in heaven or earth."

Astronauts carry their own atmosphere with them when they enter outer space. In like manner it is possible for the Christian to create his own atmosphere or climate in the soul by the constant use of the Jesus prayer. So that even though he lives in a sinful world, he will have the power to resist the world of sin which surrounds him.

In science almost every theory is tested in the laboratory. So it is with our Christian faith. It must be tested in the laboratory of life. Try this experiment. Let the last words you utter each night be the Jesus prayer. Fall asleep with these words on your lips. What better way to end a day than with Jesus? And when you wake up in the morning, let the first words you utter be the Jesus prayer. What better way to greet a new day than with Jesus? During the day, whether you are talking, sitting, walking, making something, eating or occupied in some way repeat the Jesus prayer, or the name of Jesus alone in love and adoration. Try this experiment and discover for yourself what countless others have discovered, among them Princess Illeana of Romania. She writes:

"Prayer has always been of very real importance to me, and the habit formed in early childhood of morning and evening prayer has never left me; but in the practice of the Jesus prayer I am but a beginner. I would, nonetheless, like to awaken interest in this prayer because, even if I have only touched the hem of a heavenly garment, I have touched it—and the joy is so great I would share it with others. . . ."

She tells how the Jesus prayer had been helpful to her in surgery. "Jesus," she says, had been her *last* conscious thought before she went under anesthesia, and the *first* word on her lips when she came out of surgery. It was marvellous to know, she says, that even during the operation her unconscious mind had been praying the Jesus prayer: "Lord Jesus, Son of God, have mercy upon me a sinner." For if we fall asleep with the Jesus prayer, our unconscious mind (which never sleeps) will continue to pray and we will find ourselves waking up with this prayer on our lips. This is what had happened to Princess Illeana during her surgery.

"When I arise in the morning," she continues, "it (the Jesus prayer) starts me joyfully upon a new day. When I travel by air, land, or sea, it sings within my breast. When I stand upon a platform to face my listeners, it beats encouragement. . . . At the end of a weary day, when I lay me down to rest, I give my heart over to Jesus: '(Lord), into thy hands I commend my spirit.' I sleep, but my heart, as it beats, prays on: 'Jesus.' "*

---

*H. R. H. Princess Illeana of Romania, *Introduction to the Jesus Prayer* (Cincinnati, Ohio: Forward Movement Publications).

Chapter Four

FENCING CHRIST IN

Some years ago Harold W. Ruopp wrote the following words in the *Christian Advocate*:

"The Cross having failed, the world turned to a far more subtle way of disposing of Jesus—it worshiped Him. It put Him up on a high altar with its ornate and costly symbols, and fenced Him in there. It said to Him. 'Stay there. That is where You belong. Stay there, and when Sundays come, we shall worship you.'

"And all the while Jesus keeps pleading: 'Don't fence Me in. Let Me down from your crosses. Let Me down from your altars. Let Me out of the four walls of your churches. Let Me into your minds and hearts. Let Me into your homes. Let Me into your offices and your marts of trade. Let Me into your communities and the counsels of your statesmen. I want to get back where I first started—walking in the common ways of men and talking with them about how to live, and how to live together.' "

There are many subtle ways of "fencing" Christ in. Sometimes we do it through our liturgy. The liturgy becomes a shell into which the Church withdraws, losing all contact with the world. We find Christ in the liturgy and we leave Him in the liturgy. We do not take Him out into the world with us. In church we follow the code of Christ; once we leave church we follow our own code. It's as if we lived in two different worlds, as if we were split personalities. We are one kind of person in church and another kind of person outside of church—like the ancient Hebrews whom the prophet Amos condemned. They waited anxiously for the Sabbath to come to an end so that they could go back to their cheating:

"Hear this, you who trample upon the needy...
    saying, 'When will the Sabbath be over,

that we may offer wheat for sale . . .
   and deal deceitfully with false balances,
that we may buy the poor for silver
   and the needy for a pair of sandals,
and sell the refuse of the wheat?' " (Amos 8:4–6)

They had "fenced" God in the Sabbath. They wouldn't let Him into the marketplace. And because of this the Lord said through Amos:

"I hate, I despise your feasts, and I take no delight
   in your solemn assemblies.
Even though you offer me your burnt offerings and cereal
      offerings,
   I will not accept them,
and peace offerings of your fatted beasts I will not look upon.
   Take away from me the noise of your songs;
to the melody of your harps I will not listen.
   But let justice roll down like water,
and righteousness like an everflowing stream."
                                                   (Amos 5:21–24)

Look magazine published an article entitled "Morality U.S.A." The author shows to what extent the American people have divorced morality from religion. What they do in church has *no relation whatsoever* to their everyday life. A few examples:

The French scholar, Raymond Aron, writes: "Divorce is completely accepted; freedom of sexual intercourse between young men and women is fully accepted. In sexuality, we are in revolt against Christianity."

The article tells of a highly educated, well-dressed woman who enters a Southern airport with a suitcase in each hand. A man, with Southern courtesy, starts to hold open the door for her, sees she is a Negro, and lets the door slam in her face. Is not this attitude toward the Negro a complete denial of the faith we profess in church on Sunday?

The article goes on to say that money is worshiped in our society as the root of all happiness; it is more godlike than God. How far a man will go to make money was demonstrated by Billie Sol Estes who perpetrated a multi-million-dollar swindle on his neighbors and a dozen finance companies. And yet this same Billie Sol Estes preached in church on Sunday. His religion, his worship of God, *had absolutely nothing to do* with the way he earned money. He kept Christ "fenced" in church so that He wouldn't bother him in his crooked money-making deals.

A story is told of a grocer who was also a prominent member of a church. He called downstairs, before breakfast, to his clerk:

"John, have you watered the rum?"

"Yes, sir."

"And sanded the sugar?"

"Yes, sir."

"And dusted the pepper?"

"Yes, sir."

"And chicoried the coffee?"

"Yes, sir."

"Then come up to prayers."

Nietzsche declared in 1882 that God was dead. The proof? Look at the churches, he said. They are tombs of God. "Let Me down from your crosses," says Jesus. "Let Me out of the four walls of your churches. Let Me out of your icons. Let Me into your minds and hearts."

In parts of South America it is customary with Indians starting on a long journey home from some cathedral or shrine to pause, look back into the church, and say mournfully, "Adios, Christos! Adios, Christos!" By thus saying, "Good-bye, Christ!" they leave Him in church. But it is not only South American Indians who bid Christ good-bye when they leave church. Do not many Christians today do the same? How else can we explain the great gap between what is professed in church and what is done at home or in the marketplace? In the Transfiguration Jesus did not heed the request of Peter that they remain on the mountain praying. He descended into the valley below to continue healing the sick. The purpose of our ascension through prayer and the liturgy is that we may be transfigured with Christ and then descend into the valley of life to transfigure it with His grace and love.

There is beauty in worship. There is great beauty in our liturgy and ritual. There is tradition and honor in our vestments, icons, and incense. But neither vestments nor ritual, neither liturgy nor hymns of praise, neither icons nor incense are a substitute for a dedicated heart and a consecrated life. If the heart has not yielded to Christ, if worship fails to influence our everyday life, all is empty gesture.

"Not he who *says*, 'Lord, Lord,' shall enter the kingdom of heaven, but he who does the will of my Father in heaven." To worship God with our lips and not with our lives is a lie. It is hypocrisy. And no sin did Jesus condemn more than hypocrisy.

"If you come to church," said Jesus, "and there you suddenly remember that your brother has something against you, leave church immediately and go reconcile yourself to your brother *and then come to church* and offer your gift before the altar." Take Christ out of church into your everyday human relations. Let Him reconcile you unto your brother. This is true worship. Anything less than this is a travesty.

What is religion? St. James answers, "Religion pure and undefiled before God . . . is this: to visit orphans and widows in their affliction. . . ." (James 1:27). Worship that begins and ends in church; worship that "fences" Christ in a church; worship that *does not find expression* in acts of love such as visiting orphans and widows in their afflictions, such worship is a lie.

Theodore Parker said once, "The real test of religion . . . is life. To know whom you worship, let me see you in your shop, let me overhear you in your trade; let me know how you rent your houses, how you get your money, how you keep it, or how it is spent . . . the sacramental test of your religion . . . is not the words of Jesus that you repeat; it is your week-day life, your works, and not your words."

God is with us just as much out of church as He is with us in church. We practice religion not only by what we do in church but also by what we do out of church: how we speak, how we earn our money, how we treat our wife, our husband, our employee, our children. We meet Christ in church, but we meet Him also outside of church in everyone, even in the least of our brethren: the sick, the imprisoned, the naked, the hungry, the forgotten, the lonely, the downtrodden. We come to church to *receive* Christ in Holy Communion but we receive Him in order to *take* Him out of church into the world to reshape that world according to the principles of Christ.

A latecomer asked a man who was leaving church one Sunday: "Is the liturgy over?"

He received the following answer: "According to our priest, the liturgy begins when we leave church."

Chapter Five

TEARS OF REPENTANCE

A COLLEGE PROFESSOR SAID RECENTLY that whenever the pressures and frustrations of life become severe, he puts everything aside and goes to the movies. "I find a particularly sentimental film," he says, "and I bawl like a baby."

Tears are usually the last thing a man will allow himself. Often it takes a good deal of persuasion to convince a person that crying may be the healthiest thing he can do; that a healthy cry can be the safety valve which temporarily takes care of the intense pressure within.

When we lose a loved one, psychologists tell us that it is healthy to express our sorrow in tears. Never apologize to a bereaved person for making him cry. In fact, if the bereaved person is not crying, we are told to talk about the deceased in such a way as to provoke tears. It is when sorrow is not expressed through tears that severe mental, emotional or physical illness may result.

A psychologist writes: "Crying depressurizes us emotionally, and . . . relieves stresses that may affect even our bodies."

If tears can offer us so much relief physically and emotionally, they can relieve us at least as much, if not more, in our spiritual life.

Yet, for some reason in our Christian culture we give people the impression that a good Christian does not give in to weeping. Despite the fact that Jesus wept on several occasions, we persist in creating the picture of a Christian as one who always has everything under control. In other words, if a person is really "right with God" he would not need to cry. Certainly Jesus was right with God, and yet even He found tears necessary and normal in certain times of stress.

One of the great saints of the Church writes concerning the importance of tears in our spiritual life:

"Greater than baptism itself is the fountain of tears after baptism, even though it is somewhat audacious to say so. For baptism is the washing away of evils that were in us before, but sins committed after baptism are washed away by tears. Because baptism is received in infancy, we have all defiled it, but we cleanse it anew with tears. And if God in His love for mankind had not given us tears, few indeed and hard to find would be those in a state of grace."

One of man's greatest problems today is guilt. It can take a man to the border of insanity and far beyond. It can lead to physical ailments of all kinds. It can produce an anguish far more distressing than physical pain. It can fashion sleepless nights and cheerless days without end. Guilt is one of man's greatest tormentors.

God's answer to guilt is to be found in tears—the tears of repentance.

In Luke 7:38 we read of the sinful woman who came to Jesus. "Weeping . . . she began to wet our Lord's feet with her tears and wiped them with the hair of her head." To this woman who grieved so much for her sinful life Jesus said, "Thy sins are forgiven thee"—washed away by the tears of repentance.

Of our Lord's apostles perhaps none was more devoted to Jesus than Peter. He boasted that he would under all circumstances remain loyal to his Lord and Master, even at the threat of death. Yet this same Peter vehemently denied his Lord. Three times he swore that he didn't know Jesus. Then suddenly "Peter remembered the saying of Jesus, 'Before the cock crows you will deny me three times.' And he went out and wept bitterly" (Matt. 26:75). He didn't just weep, says the Gospel, he wept *bitterly.* He was baptized a second time; this time by his own tears of repentance. Because he wept so bitterly his sin was forgiven and later he was given even "the keys to the kingdom of heaven."

If Peter's tears brought him such great forgiveness, surely our tears can do the same for us. Whether it be your heart that cries or your eyes, let your tears be not tears of despair, not tears of self-pity, not tears of hurt pride, but tears of repentance that lead to salvation. When we look at the cross we see what sin did to God. We see also what sin made God do to save us. If nothing else moves us to shed tears of repentance, certainly the sight of God on the cross should.

Leslie Weatherhead tells a legend from the war, probably an old one from other wars. There was an English mother who had a particularly gifted son who gave his life on the battlefield. He was brilliant, had led his classes in scholarship and made a remarkable record in Oxford. He went to war and was killed in action. Then his mother had a strange dream. She dreamed that an angel came to her and told her that she might have her son back for five minutes.

"Choose," said the angel. "What five minutes will you have? Will it be in the hour of his high honor in Oxford, or in the hour of his heroism in battle?"

The mother did not even hesitate. She said, "If I can have him back for five minutes, I prefer to have him, not when he was in Oxford, not when he was in war. I would like to have him as a little boy on a certain day when he had disobeyed me. He had run into the garden, angry and rebellious. Then pretty soon he came back and threw himself into my arms and said he was sorry. His face was hot and red. His eyes were filled with tears. He looked so small and so precious. I saw his love in his eyes and felt his love in his body pressed close to mine—and how my love went out to him at that moment! If I can have him back again for just five minutes, let me have him as a dear little repentant boy."

There can be no doubt that tears of repentance bring the greatest joy to our Father's heart. "There is great joy in heaven," said Jesus, "over one sinner who repents."

Amongst all those who mourn, none shall be sooner consoled than those who mourn for their own sins. Our Lord promised this when He said, "Blessed are those who mourn, for *they shall be comforted*." They shall be comforted with a peace and joy that pass all human understanding.

Lent is, among other things, a time for tears, tears that relieve us of the great burden of guilt; tears that lead to confession; tears that cleanse, re-baptize, and make us new persons in Christ.

There is an old legend according to which God said to

one of His angels: "Go down to earth and bring back the most precious thing in the world."

The angel flew down to earth and traversed hills and valley, seas and rivers, in search of the most precious thing in the world. Finally after a number of years, the angel came upon a battlefield and beheld a brave soldier dying of the wounds he had received in defense of his country. The angel seized a drop of blood, brought it to the throne of God, and said, "Lord God, surely this is the most precious thing in the world." God said "Indeed, O angel, this is precious in my sight, but it is not the most precious thing in the world."

So the angel returned to earth and, after many years of wandering, came to a hospital where a nurse lay dying of a dread disease that she had contracted through nursing others. As the last breath passed from her lifeless form, the angel caught it up and brought it to the throne of judgment, saying, "O Lord God, surely this is the most precious thing in the world." God smiled at the angel and said, "Indeed, O angel, sacrifice in behalf of others is very precious in my sight, but it is not the most precious thing in the world."

The angel returned to earth and this time wandered for many years. Then it happened that the angel beheld one day a vicious looking man riding through a dark forest. He was going to the hut of his enemy to destroy him. As he approached the enemy's house, light streamed from the windows as the members of the household, unsuspecting, went about their tasks. The villian approached and looked into the window. There he saw the wife putting the little son to bed, teaching him to pray, instructing him to thank God for all His blessings. As the vicious man looked at this scene, he forgot why he had come. He remembered his own childhood—how his mother had put him to bed and taught him to pray to God. The man's heart melted and a tear rolled down his cheek. The angel caught the tear and flew to God saying, "Dear Lord, surely this is the most precious thing in the world—the tear of repentance."

God beamed upon the angel as He spoke, "Indeed, O angel, you have brought me the most precious thing in the world— the tear of repentance which opens the gates of heaven."

Chapter Six

MIND THE LIGHT!

THE KEEPER OF A LIGHTHOUSE in France was boasting of the brilliance of his lamp. Asked what would happen if the lamp went out, he replied, "Impossible! Yonder in the darkness there are ships sailing to every harbor in the world. If this light went out tonight, who knows how many of those vessels might be shipwrecked. I like to think that the eyes of the whole world are fixed on my light."

In a similar way the eyes of the whole world are fixed on the follower of Christ. Jesus said in today's Gospel, "You are the light of the world." You are as a city set on a hill, whose light shines far out into the darkness. You are as a candle set on a candlestick to give light to all those about you. "Let your light so shine before men, that they may see your good works and glorify your Father who is in heaven."

A little boy sat one night at the desk in his room, his pudgy nose pressed against the window as he looked out into the street. He was watching a lamplighter going up and down the streets lighting the old gas street lamps. His mother called him for dinner. He didn't hear. She called him a second time; still he didn't come. When a third call was necessary, the mother went to his room and found him absorbed in the lamplighter. Seeing his mother, he said, "Look! Look! There is a man out there punching holes in the darkness!"

The Lord Jesus tells us that He expects every Christian to be a lamplighter punching holes in the darkness. But *where* and *how*, we ask, are we to punch holes in the darkness of today's world?

In the first place, we must show concern for the spiritual life of our fellow man. A little boy who lost his birth certificate on his way to school, tearfully told his teacher, "I've lost my excuse for being born." There are many people in the

world today—some of them may be our own friends or rela-
tives—who have lost their excuse for being born. Life has no
meaning for them. They are lost to Christ and the Church.

We have a solemn responsibility to attract these people to
Christ and His Church. If they had polio and we had the cure
for polio, wouldn't it be criminal on our part to refuse to
share the cure with them? Is it less criminal for us to withhold
from them who dwell in darkness Christ who is the Light of
the world? I know of one of our parishioners who said to a friend,
"You know, I have missed seeing you in church." This person
was flattered to know that there was someone who missed him
when he did not attend the liturgy on Sunday. Since then he
has been attending the liturgy faithfully with his family. All
it took was a show of kind, personal concern on the part of a
friend.

The greatest gift that any man can give to another is Christ.
Very few people pass even a single day without being in touch
with someone who does not know Christ, but who greatly needs
to know Him. I know that we sometimes hesitate to speak to
others about Christ. But let us remember that when we speak
to others about Christ and the Church we are not asking them
to follow us. We are asking them to follow Christ. "Evangelism,"
writes C. T. Niles, "is just one beggar telling another beggar
where to find bread." *You are the light of the world.*

Another area where we need light today is in the home.
The influence of the home never dies; it lives on in the children and in their children. It was a home that produced the
late President John F. Kennedy and it was a home that produced Lee Harvey Oswald. Instead of bemoaning the darkness
that exists in the home today, it is much better to light a
candle. The most brilliant candle we can light in the home is
the shining example of Christian parents. Children need parents they can admire, parents they can honor, parents they
can imitate and use as patterns, parents who have a living relationship with God, parents who put Christ first in their lives,
parents who realize the importance of prayer in the home,
parents who live an honest, sincere Christian life, who worship
Christ in church every Sunday. Such parents leave their children the finest possible legacy—an example that will serve as

an inspiration to them for the rest of their lives. "You are the light of the world," said Jesus. If we are to be lights for Jesus in this world, the first place to begin shining is in the home.

Another area where the world needs the light of Christ today is in our work, in the business world. One can boast that he is the best Christian in the world, but if he cheats at work, if he is not dependable, if he does not turn out the best possible work, he is a poor witness for Christ.

There are far too many Christians today who leave Christ in church, who refuse to take Him to work with them. The result is that what goes on in church for an hour and fifteen minutes on Sunday morning has nothing to do with what goes on in business the rest of the week.

If a Christian is a carpenter, he must be the best possible carpenter. If he is an engineer, he is to be the best possible engineer. If he is a cook, he is to be the best possible cook. "You are the light of the world."

"That you may be blameless and innocent," writes St. Paul to the Philippians, "the sons of God in the midst of a crooked and perverse nation, among whom you shine as lights in the world." We live in a world whose moral standards have descended to the level of the animal. It is easy to conform to the darkness of the world. After all, few people want to be different, odd, eccentric. But for the sake of Christ we must be different. "We must obey God rather than man," said the apostle Peter. We must be out of tune with music of the streets because as Christians we march to the rhythm of a different drummer: Christ. *"You are the light of the world."*

We need to shine as lights for Christ in the darkness of suffering. A deeply dedicated Christian was told one day that he was incurably ill with cancer. He wrote a testimony which reveals how the light of his Christian faith dispelled the darkness of despair from his heart. I share with you part of his testimony:

"When I read that cancer is man's worst enemy, I am not so sure. I do not think God allows enemies to prevail; rather He seems to use the things we dread to draw us closer to Him.

"Since we must all die, God seems kindly when He sends a messenger in advance with a gentle but emphatic warning. Surely we can all use a little time to get ready for Judgment. The realization that one has cancer sharpens one's whole outlook on life; the earth is more beautiful, the sky a little clearer, and every moment of the day a thing to be hoarded. . . .

"Whether we are well or sick, we are God's children, deeply loved and providentially guarded. . . .

"Death is not the end but the beginning of the only life which can satisfy the restless, limitless, glorious cravings of the human soul."

Jesus said, "In the world you have tribulation, but be of good cheer, I have overcome the world." How well these words of our Lord are exemplified through the faith of this one Christian afflicted with cancer. His testimony is indeed a light of inspiration. *"You are the light of the world."*

"But," you ask, *"how* can I be a light for Christ in my home, in my work, in my suffering to those who have lost their excuse for being born, to the world about me?"

Perhaps this story will help. It is called "Recipe for Shining." A GI brought back from Germany a little phosphorescent match case that illuminates in the darkness. One evening, in a company of friends, he took it out to show them. He turned out all the lights, but the obstinate little match case would not shine. The GI concluded that he had been swindled. The next day, while examining his purchase more closely, he read on one side, "If you wish me to shine, keep me in the sunlight." He followed the directions, put it out where the sun's rays could be absorbed and then in a dark room found it had a brilliant glow.

We cannot be lights for Christ in this world unless we live in His presence day by day exposing ourselves to the light of His teachings and grace through prayer, the Gospel, the liturgy and the Sacraments. Only then can we be what Jesus intends us to be: lights shining in the darkness.

Let me share with you this personal story of a woman who was married to a lighthouse keeper.

"I was living at Sandy Hook when I first met my husband. He took me to that lighthouse as his bride. I enjoyed the life there, for the lighthouse was on land and we could have a garden and raise flowers. But one day the Government transferred us to the Light on Robin's reef, surrounded totally by water. The day came when I said to him, 'I can't stay here; the sight of water wherever I look makes me too lonesome.' I refused to unpack my trunk and boxes, but somehow they seemed to get unpacked and I've been here ever since. It is almost forty years.

"One night my husband caught a bad cold while tending the light. It turned into pneumonia and he died. We buried him on the mainland over there. Every morning when the sun comes up, I stand at this porthole and look toward his grave. Sometimes the hills are brown, sometimes they are green, sometimes they are white with snow. But they always bring a message from him—something I have heard him say more often than anything else—just three words: 'Mind the light!' "

And this is exactly what Jesus tells us: Mind the light! You are not to be influenced by the climate in which you live. As My followers and disciples, you are to be climate makers in your homes, in your businesses, in your suffering, in the world. "You are the light of the world. . . . Let your light so shine before men, that they may see your good works and give glory to your Father who is in heaven."

Chapter Seven

"I BELIEVE..."

HERE ARE TWO VERY FAMILIAR WORDS—the first two words of the Nicene Creed: "*I believe....*" We say them every Sunday when we confess the creed during the liturgy. "I believe in one God, Father Almighty...." What do they mean, if anything? Why do we keep repeating them Sunday after Sunday?

Note the first word: "*I* believe...." Belief is something personal, something existential, something you must do yourself, something nobody else can do *for* you. No one will ever get to heaven on someone else's faith. My mother may have been a great believer, but I'll never coast into heaven on her faith. My uncle may have been a great bishop of the church, but this has nothing to do with me and my relationship to Christ. This is something personal—exceedingly personal. "*I* believe...." Not my mother, not my father, not my uncle, not my sponsor in baptism, but "*I* believe...."

We read in the Old Testament that Jacob wrestled with God. We are to understand from this story that a great thing happened in the life of Jacob. Somewhere in his career he underwent a conversion, an experience with God. At the same point in his life this ambitious man was truly blessed and touched by God's grace. As a result of this very personal experience with God his life was changed. The new name, Israel, given to Jacob at this point signifies the new person he became.

Just as Jacob had a personal "struggle" with God, a personal meeting with Him, so each and every one of us must meet Christ personally and decide for Him at some point in life. An eminent theologian of our church, the Rev. Dr. John Meyendorff, writes:

"We are told in the Gospels that religious education implies a positive acceptance of Christ. This is the real conversion.

If this marriage does not take place at some time during the life of a Christian, he is simply not a Christian. We have a very clear statement about this in the tradition of the Fathers. What makes a Christian a Christian is this personal commitment to Christ. *One's formal belonging to the church through baptism and other sacramental participation remains a mere potential if the individual commitment does not take place.* The sacramental gifts of Baptism and Eucharist and of all the sacraments are essential for an objective membership in the body of Christ; but again they are pure potentials if they are not taken seriously and if a conversion of the heart and mind does not occur at some point in one's life." *

When we were baptized our sponsor was the one who renounced Satan and accepted Christ for us. He was the one who confessed the "I believe" of the Nicene Creed for us. But if we are to be true Christians, there must come a time in life when we must say these words for ourselves—a time when we ourselves decide for Christ and commit our whole being to Him as personal Lord and Saviour. Unless this happens we are Christians *in name only*.

What does it mean to "believe" in Christ? To answer this question the Danish philosopher Kierkegaard uses the illustration of a poor swimmer who wants to keep a toe on the bottom rather than trust himself to the water. But he is not really a swimmer until he "ventures far out," abandoning the support of the bottom. Faith is like lying on "70,000 fathoms of water," he says, relying solely on the buoyancy of the sea.

Kierkegaard calls this the "leap of faith." In order for the leap of faith to occur one must first come to an awareness of his finitude, of his insufficiency, of his powerlessness, of his emptiness, of his aloneness. This may happen through sin, guilt, failure, death, alcoholism, sickness, insecurity, despair. One is suddenly brought face to face with the fact that he cannot maintain this "toehold" on the bottom of the sea, that he must make the "leap of faith," that he must trust the buoyancy of the sea. And when he does, he experiences the glorious freedom of casting off onto 70,000 fathoms of water

---

* "Orthodox Christian Education Commission," Bulletin No. 2, Vol. VII, Summer, 1963.

knowing that he is supported not by his own toehold but by God.

A further illustration of this is found in the story of the little girl who asked her father if she could go down to him in the cellar. He said that she might. But when about to descend she found that the ladder had been taken away. "I cannot get down," she called; "there is no ladder." "Jump down," said the father, "and I will catch you. My arms are wide open." The girl had faith in her father. She jumped unhesitatingly into the darkness, and was safely caught in her father's arms.

When I say *"I believe,"* I mean that I believe not only with my *mind* which tells me my Father is down there waiting for me, but also with my *will* which makes me take the leap of faith into His waiting arms. And it is a continuous leap. No one can say with satisfaction, "I made the leap last year. Now I have landed on the other side. Now I have faith." Even if in some crisis I conquered my fears, the next threat may find me vulnerable again. So faith is a continuous leap to God who makes His riches, His strength, His guidance constantly available to us.

To say "I believe in Christ" is to believe in a Christ who lives today. So long as Christ is somebody, even a very important somebody, who lived many centuries ago, I have less to do with Him than with many people whom I meet today. This is not the kind of Christ I believe in. The kind of Christ I believe in lives today. He speaks to me today. He is present with me today. He forgives me today. He guides me today. He loves me today. He judges me today. He is a contemporary Christ.

When a Christian says "I believe in God," he does not claim to understand everything about God. Mrs. Einstein was asked once if she understood her husband's theory of relativity. "No," she said, "I don't understand his theory of relativity, but *I know my husband.*" In like manner, I, as a Christian, do not understand everything about God, "whose ways are not my ways," but I *know* God. I know Him in Christ. I know that He loves me. I know that He came down from heaven for me. I know that He gave His life for me. In view of all this, I can safely trust that no matter what He

allows to come to me, there is meaning and purpose and love
behind it: God's meaning, God's purpose, and God's love.

"I believe," said the apostles. They made the leap of faith
into Christ's arms. Listen to the record of what their faith
accomplished:

They "who through faith subdued kingdoms, wrought
righteousness, obtained promises, stopped the mouths of lions,
quenched the violence of fire, escaped the edge of the sword,
out of weakness were made strong, walked valiant in fight, and
turned to flight the armies of the aliens."

"*I believe. . . ,*" said the woman of Samaria. She made the
leap of faith to Christ. We ask her, "How did the Lord Jesus
treat you?" She answers, "He gave me the water of life of
which 'if any man drink he shall never thirst again.' "

"*I believe. . . ,*" said the penitent thief. He made the leap
of faith. We ask him: "How did the Lord Jesus treat you?"
He answers, "He told me that I would dwell in the house of
the Lord forever."

"*I believe. . . ,*" said the adulteress. She made the leap of
faith to Christ. We ask her, "How did the Lord Jesus treat
you?" She answers, "He lifted the burden of my sin. He restored my soul. He made we whiter than snow."

Chapter Eight

"HE THAT HAS EARS, LET HIM HEAR"

A MAN COMPLAINED that his wife just talked, talked and talked all the time. "What does she talk about?" asked a friend. "That's just the trouble," sighed the man, "she doesn't say!"

Talk, it is said, is cheap. Often it says nothing worth hearing. The reason lies largely in the fact that if we took time to listen and learn great truths, we might then have something worth saying. A good listener is not only popular but after a while he knows something. Someone once asked an old Vermont farmer why he spoke so seldom. "Well," he drawled, "the Lord gave us two ears and one mouth, didn't He? Reckon He knew what He was doing."

In any argument, while the first person is speaking the second person is usually so busy thinking what he will say in rebuttal that he almost never fully listens to the other's point of view. How different it would be if we really listened as others spoke. Perhaps then we would understand!

Good listening is conducive to good human relations! A prominent psychologist conducted weekly classes in sympathetic listening for the foremen of a large industry. The foremen then began holding private conferences with disgruntled employees, during which the employee was encouraged to do all the talking. The result was that the worker in almost every case ended up by admitting there were two sides to the problem. By listening to each other, each side was able to gain understanding. And once there was understanding, it was not too difficult to come to a satisfactory solution. How different our labor relations would be if management listened to labor and labor to management.

How different our home life would be, how much more serene, if children would *listen* to parents and parents to children. We parents have the bad habit of not listening to our children. How often we tell them, "Keep still. You're too young. You don't know anything!" Thus we crush their budding individuality; we instill in them a feeling of inferiority and we tear down the lines of communication between us.

Taylor Caldwell's novel, *The Listener*, is based on the fact that no one seems to have time to listen to others, except the very few who have made it their profession. Parents have no time to hear what the children say. The children seem to have no time to hear what the parents have to say. Husbands and wives have no time to listen to each other.

How different marriage would be, how much happier, if the husband would *listen* to the wife and the wife to the husband. How much understanding would be gained! How much insight! And how many serious tragedies avoided. For in listening we give ourselves to others, we give them our attention, we commit ourselves to them. Unless two people listen to each other, a relationship cannot grow between them. Each will be a stranger to the other.

Most people feel alone in their problems. Let them find someone who will *listen* to them, who will try to understand how they feel, and they begin to experience the beginnings of a fellowship in the most isolated part of their life. The problem no longer seems so unbearable; someone in a small way is sharing it.

Kind listening is always an expression of Christian love. Often people need a *compassionate ear* more than they need a cheerful word. A person who has severe inner conflicts needs to talk. To such a person talk is therapeutic. For by talking he unburdens himself of some of the tension. The greatest act of Christian charity toward such a person is to sit with him and *listen to him*. Many times people will come to you and say, "Gee, thanks. You don't know how much you've helped me." And you sit there afterwards thinking, "What did I do? I didn't do anything. What happened?" This is what you did; you reached out across this great area of desolation and you held his hand for a while. You didn't give him a lot of advice. You gave him a chance to catch his breath and figure out for himself what he was going to do. *You listened to him!*

In treating emotionally ill patients, Freud became dis-

gusted with both electrotherapy and hypnotism. He simply began listening to his patients talk out their problems. From this
seemingly inauspicious beginning came psychotherapy.

Psychiatrists understand fully the value of listening. They
charge anywhere from $25 to $100 an hour for listening. And
good listening, they say, is not easy. It is hard work.

The story is told of an old psychiatrist and a young one.
Both had offices in the same building. At five o'clock each day
when the younger psychiatrist got on the elevator, wilted and
bedraggled, he would see the older one calmly smoking a cigar
—everything just so—standing there with quiet expectation of
arriving at the main floor, getting into his car and being driven
home. And the younger psychiatrist kept thinking: What does
he have that I don't have? How can he handle all of this with
composure, compassion and tranquility? Finally one day he
got up nerve enough to ask, "May I speak to you just for a
minute, doctor? Each day when I see you get on the elevator
you look immaculate and serene. Yet I know you've had a
busy schedule. When I get on the elevator, I'm just bushed.
How can you sit there and listen to people all day long, telling
you all their troubles, and not let it bother you?" Whereupon
the older psychiatrist said, "Who listens?"

Is not this the cry of those who suffer, "Who listens?"

There are different kinds of listening. There is the listening
of criticism; there is the listening of resentment. There is the
listening of superiority; there is the listening of indifference.
There is the listening of the man who only listens because for
the moment he cannot get a chance to speak. But to listen attentively takes love. There is no greater way to depersonalize
another than not to listen when he speaks. It's like telling him
in no uncertain terms, "You are nothing to me. You mean
nothing to me." On the other hand, to listen to a person attentively is to make him feel that he is a person—a person who
is appreciated and loved.

To listen to our fellow man is important, but to listen to
the voice of God is even more important. "He that has ears,
let him hear," says Jesus. He tells us how people listen to
the Word of God. He likens the Word of God to seed. Some
falls along the path and is stepped upon. Some falls on rocky

ground and withers. Some falls among thorns and is choked. And some falls on good soil and yields a hundredfold. It is amazing what God can do with our life if we will listen to His Word.

A short time ago we read in the newspapers of three men flying in a private plane. Suddenly the pilot died of a heart attack. The plane went out of control and began spinning down toward earth and certain death. Just then, one of the passengers grabbed the two-way radio and called for help. Just as quickly a voice from the airport answered and gave instructions which were carefully followed. The plane landed safely and three thankful passengers emerged. They had escaped death. A voice had come through at the right moment to meet their need.

Such a voice speaks to us today in the words of Jesus. It tells us how we can be saved from sin and eternal death. It tells us how to live the abundant life. It is the voice of One who is "the way, the truth, and the life." It gives purpose, direction, and meaning to life. "He that has ears," says Jesus, "let him hear." Listen to the highest and the best in life. Listen to the voice of God and then listen kindly and attentively to your fellow man.

Chapter Nine

"YOUR MARRIAGE: DUEL OR DUET?"

"I HAD A PECULIAR FEELING as I saw his skis flashing through the water, and when he climbed upon the dock and I saw his broad shoulders and engaging smile I knew that I loved him. He was the man for me."

Dr. Wayne J. Anderson tells us that this romantic and emotionally stirring statement was made by an intelligent college girl as she recounted a recent experience at Lake Minnetonka. The man in question? She had never seen him before and has not seen him since this memorable occasion. Still, within her heart, she knows that he is her man. She is certain that some inexplicable fate will soon bring them together. They will marry. Their home will be a picturesque rambler with a station wagon and a convertible in its garages, and a sparkling swimming pool in its back yard. Their union will be blessed with healthy, happy children and life together will be glorious. All they need to do to lead to this heavenly existence is to get married!

Isn't this the kind of thinking about marriage that is prevalent today not only among teen-agers but also among many adults who should know better? They look upon happiness in marriage as something that occurs automatically as soon as they turn their backs to the altar. They expect the mere saying of "I do" to assure them marital happiness served on a silver platter.

Does anyone learn to play the piano immediately? We may learn to bring forth a few agreeable sounds in five minutes, but we know that it takes hard work and strenuous practice to produce really worthwhile music. The same is true with successful marriages. They don't happen in minutes. It takes time. It takes years of real love and persistent effort and patient understanding to produce a happy marriage. No two people are completely compatible when they are first married. Compatibility is the achievement of marriage. One must work for it. As the great psychiatrist, Dr. Carl G. Jung, said, "Seldom, or perhaps never, does a marriage develop into an individual relationship smoothly and without crisis; there is no coming to consciousness without pain." And one of the deepest pains in life is the crucifixion of self—nailing it to the cross of a higher purpose than ourselves, namely, the success of our marriage, the happiness of our mate and children. Nothing stands in the way of a happy marriage as much as self: thinking of oneself instead of the person loved, complaining of our not being loved instead of loving; waiting for others to serve us instead of going out of *our* way to serve those we love. In marriage we must live "in honour preferring one another" (Rom. 12:10, I Pet. 3:7). We have not married to insure the happiness of ourselves alone, but equally, if not more, to seek the happiness of the other. Love "seeketh not her own" (I Cor. 13:5). Love seeks the glory and the happiness of the other.

What a difference there would be in marriage if, in the words of St. Francis, we would try:

"... not so much ... to be consoled as to console;
(not so much) to be understood as to understand;
(not so much) to be loved as to love."

We hear much talk today about the Berlin Wall. We forget that in many marriages there is a wall that is even more impenetrable than the Berlin Wall. The wall in marriage is built not of rocks but of little misunderstandings that are allowed to accumulate. Quarrels will occur in marriage, more for some than for others, but this does not mean that our marriage is a failure. A broken bone, for example, may be stronger than before the breakage, if it heals properly. But there is one thing we must never do with our misunderstandings. We must never allow them to accumulate. There is a verse in the Bible which says, "Don't let the sun go down on your wrath." Applied to married couples it means, "If you've had differences of opinion, don't let the day vanish into night without talking about these differences and asking each other's forgiveness." Otherwise the resentments accumulate day after day and soon a wall rises in the home—a wall so high that it can no longer be taken down. And, as invariably happens, the husband finds himself living on one side of the wall and the wife on the other, with no communication between them. So in marriage take the advice of the Apostle Paul: never—never—let "the sun go down on your wrath."

Another great source of irritation in marriage is *nagging*. I read this saying recently: "She used to knit for him but now she needles." From seemingly harmless words, endlessly repeated, comes fatal and bitter tension.

Solomon said, "It is better to live on the corner of a rooftop than in a house shared by a contentious woman" (Prov. 21:9). He echoed this thought when he said, "A continual dripping on a rainy day and a contentious woman are alike" (Prov. 27:15). It was an Oriental torture to bind a man and let water drip upon his head, not torrentially, but lightly and insistently until he became insane. The ungracious little habit of nagging can cause any person to lose his mental balance.

A wife once said to her husband: "I can read you like a book, John." "Why don't you, then?" replied the husband. "You skip what you don't like in a book but in me you linger over it." We linger over it! We are not content with criticizing others for something they should have done or something they should not have done. There is a time to speak of that. But we continue to speak of it. We drag yesterday and yesterday back into today. We take pleasure in reopening wounds. We seem to take pathological delight in keeping an unhappy experience alive. Even the law says that a man cannot be tried twice for the same crime. No child, no parent, no husband, no wife should ever be tried for the same misdemeanor twice. Jesus speaks of forgiveness as something conclusive. There is an end to it. And there must be an end to the unforgiving spirit of nagging if marriage is to prosper.

What a difference there would be if, instead of nagging, we tried again to make the other half of the prayer of St. Francis a reality in our marriage:

> "Lord, make me an instrument of Your peace.
> Where there is hatred, let me sow love;

> Where there is injury, pardon;
> Where there is doubt, faith;
> Where there is despair, hope;
> Where there is sadness, joy."

Ralph Sockman has written:

"In my boyhood community we had a colloquial expression for courtship. It would be said, 'John is paying attention to Mary.' He paid attention to everything she did and said. He watched her at parties. He thought of her during the day and dreamed of her at night. He wrote letters to her. He sent her flowers and candy. Thus, because he paid attention to her, he came to win her affection and love."

We win a person's love when we pay attention to him or her. But what happens after marriage? Do we continue to "pay attention" to each other? Where are the words of tenderness? What happens to the vocabulary of love? Where are the little kindnesses to each other, the thoughtful remembrances?

Love would never die if, even after marriage, we kept paying attention to our loved one; if we would express our love and let our partner know that he or she is loved and appreciated; if we would lubricate the differences or creaks in marriage with the oil of love; if we would forgive each other daily never allowing our resentments to grow into insurmountable walls; if we would try not to keep re-opening old wounds. How different marriage would be if only we "paid attention" to the one we love.

According to an ancient legend there once lived on a remote island an odd kind of bird. Each bird had only one wing and therefore could not fly. Some birds had the wing on the right side, some on the left. On the side opposite its wing each bird had a hooklike growth. In time the birds discovered that when a bird found a partner that had a wing on the other side, they could hold on to each other by locking their hooklike growth and soar high into the air. Only the birds that found an adventuresome mate were able to get off the island and fly aloft. All others had to remain forever on the ground.

The legend seems to have been invented to illustrate the thrilling opportunities of married life. When a man or woman finds a suitable mate, when they love each other and forgive each other and appreciate each other, then it is that they experience one of the profoundest joys in life. They experience the happiness of working, playing, planning, worshipping together. They lift each other, console each other, strengthen each other, cheer each other, inspire each other. It is no wonder that God said on the day of creation: "It is not good that man should be alone; I will make an help meet for him."

A physician met a husband outside the operating room one day and said, "My friend, I need courage to tell you this. Your wife can live only three weeks."

Later the husband said, "I tried to cram into those three weeks all the happiness I should have put into twenty years." Why cram happiness into weeks when by inviting Christ into our home every day, the happiness of marriage can be shared and spread out to last a lifetime?

Chapter Ten

PERSONS OR THINGS?

A MOTHER IN TRENTON, N.J., left her month-old baby in its carriage in her yard while she went to answer the phone.

There was no reason to be afraid for the child's safety, the mother felt, as she would be gone only a few minutes. But when she returned she was horrified to find two small boys, each about five years old, using her infant for a football. They were tossing the child in the air and kicking it about.

The mother screamed and rescued the child which was by now in critical condition. It was taken to the hospital with multiple skull fractures.

When questioned by the police, the boys seemed very bewildered by the whole affair. They said they had thought that the child was a doll!

It is almost unbelievable that two children would mistake an infant for a doll. Yet it is even more unbelievable that we adults in our everyday relations with people mistake *persons* for *things*. We treat persons as things. We play with them as if they were "dolls." We "use" them for our own pleasure, profit and exploitation. Erich Fromm writes in his book, *The Sane Society*:

"What is modern man's relationship to his fellow man? It is one between two abstractions, two living machines, who use each other. The employer uses the ones whom he employs; the salesman uses his customers. Everybody is to everybody else a commodity, always to be treated with certain friendliness, because even if he is not of use now, he may be later." *

We forget sometimes that the curse of Communism which plagues the world today was born as a reaction against the use of man by man for profit. The peasant became a tool, a ma-

---

* Fromm, Erich, *The Sane Society* (Holt, Rinehart and Winston, Inc.).

chine, an instrument in the hands of the landlord to help make more profit. The important thing was not the peasant but profit. Immanuel Kant, the great philosopher, believed that the greatest immorality was to use another person as a means to an end.

Reuel Howe said once that God created us as persons to be loved, not as things to be used. And yet how many times do we do the opposite? We love things and use persons. We consider people as pieces of toast to be buttered up and then we wonder why our relations are so crummy.

Dr. Victor Frankl tells that when the prisoners entered the Nazi concentration camps they were deprived of all their possessions and were assigned a number. These numbers were often tattooed on their skin, and also had to be sewn to a certain spot on the trousers, jacket or coat. The prisoner was never again referred to by his name but only by his number. It was as if he had lost his personality and become a thing.

Consider how the person is treated as a thing in the business world. Just as one oils machines, business uses advertising to oil people with the constant repetition of slogans by newspapers, radio, television. Psychology, psychiatry and psychoanalysis are used as tools to manipulate people, to motivate them to buy certain products. The important thing is not the person—or what the product or the advertising does to the person—but the selling of the product. The person becomes merely a thing to be exploited.

Is not the same true in real estate? For many people today the important thing is not the person but the property value. If the property value goes down when a minority person moves into the neighborhood, then I will not sell to a minority person, so say some people. The important thing is not the person— the family that is hurt by prejudice—the important value is a thing—the property!

And how about our sex morals? Some time ago Clare Boothe Luce wrote an article in one of our national magazines entitled, "The 'Love Goddess' Who Never Found Any Love." It was about the suicide of a famous actress. Mrs. Luce explained that one of the main complaints of this actress was that as a sex symbol she became a thing. "I just hate to be a thing," she said. In the same article a newspaper editor indicted certain motion picture producers for turning "woman into a piece of meat." Archbishop William Temple said once, "To use sex ... as an opportunity of passing amusement always involves treating another person as a plaything or toy."

Modern literature voices great protest against those forces in modern culture that would turn man into a thing. Hemingway, Yeats, Faulkner, T. S. Eliot, the Existentialists—all try to assert that man is more than a mere thing that is pushed about in the universe. Man, they say, is a person who creates his own destiny and meaning.

But the greatest protest against the turning of man into a thing is voiced by Christ. "Truly, I say to you, as you did it to one of the least of these my brethren, you did it to me." Jesus tells us here that He is constantly walking this earth as the hidden Christ, meeting us again and again in the hungry, the homeless, the lonely, the imprisoned, the destitute. No person is a thing. Every person is the hidden Christ. In every person we meet Christ. As we treat that person we treat Christ. What greater compliment could Christ pay man?

Every person, says the Apostle Paul, is "the brother for whom Christ died"—not a thing, not a tool, not the means of production, not a tenant, not a customer, not a "piece of meat," not an IBM card—but the brother, the sister, "for whom Christ died."

In Mark 8:22–25 we read that Jesus once cured a blind man. He touched the man's eyes and asked him whether he saw anything. The man answered, "I see men; but they look like trees, walking." The man received vision but it was blurred. He saw persons as if they were things. Then Jesus touched the man's eyes again and he saw clearly.

Christ can always perform the miracle of clearing the blurred vision we have of our fellow man so that we may see him no longer as a mere thing to be exploited and used, but as the person for whom Christ died, the person in whom we meet the hidden Christ today.

Dr. Paul Tournier in his book, *A Doctor's Casebook*, states that in the Bible there are whole pages of names. He insists that this is the proof that the Bible thinks of people first and foremost not as numbers, or ideas, or cases, but as persons. "The proper name," says Dr. Tournier, "is the symbol of the person. If I forget my patients' names, if I say to myself, 'Ah! There's that gall bladder type or that consumptive that I saw the other day,' I am interesting myself more in their gall bladder or their lungs than in themselves as persons." He insists that a person must be always a person, and never a case.

Jesus never dealt with people as another case of leprosy, another case of doubt, another case of adultery or bereavement or poverty. In his mind these were persons, each loved and respected as an individual—a *person* troubled with leprosy, a *person* troubled with doubt or adultery. In His love and respect for persons, Jesus was showing how God feels about people.

How many people there are today who feel that nobody is really interested in them as persons. Nobody opens himself up to them in a personal way. They feel lost, abandoned! In a world that is so full of push-buttons, so impersonal, the love of God for each individual needs to be made personal to people. And it can be done if the love of Christ dwells in each one of us. A physician, speaking of a large hospital in Germany, said, "I think I can say that my hospital is pervaded by a personal spirit, but I believe we owe this almost entirely to a single person—our Sister Superior, who is so profoundly human that everyone whose life she touches feels that he is considered a person, feels himself becoming a person."

What was this Sister Superior's secret? The physician went on to explain that it was in her personal communion with Christ. She received so much love from Christ that she lavished it on all whom she met, making each one feel that he was a person loved not only by the Sister Superior but also by God.

I close with these words by Horace Wood because they summarize well all we have said: "Before Christ, a man loves things and uses people. After Christ, he loves people and uses things."

"Truly I say to you, as you did it to one of the least of these my brethren, you did it to me."

Chapter Eleven

"HE IS ABLE..."
THE ADEQUATE CHRIST

OUR CHRISTIAN RELIGION has been telling us through the ages that God is all-powerful. In the last few decades science has been demonstrating just *how* all-powerful God is. For example:

In one cup of cold water there is enough power to propel a ship across the Atlantic Ocean.

The submarine "Nautilus" can travel at the rate of twenty-five knots night and day for a whole year and all the power necessary for that year will have been released from 26.15 pounds of uranium 235, which a person could hold in the palm of his hand.

A prominent physicist tells us that if we were to pay the light bill of the sun, pay for its energy at one penny per kilowatt, that a one-hundredth-millionth part of a second would cost us more than World War II. This is power—God's power. We use it every day and most of us just take it for granted.

Man invents a pump to lift water from the earth, yet he carries a pump inside him that pumps ceaselessly, night and day, without repair, without attention, for seventy or eighty years, lifting two hundred and eighty thousand tons of blood a year, and so silently the doctor has to listen to it with a stethoscope.

If we could possibly assemble one gram of electrons and release their power, we could pull a train of loaded freight cars six thousand miles long at 30 miles per hour for slightly more than a half hour or a distance of about fifteen miles. The most powerful engines man can make are weak when compared to the power of God in nature.

Everywhere nature speaks of the power of God. Now we have a faint idea of what our Lord meant when He said, "All power is given unto me in heaven and in earth."

Is it only in nature that God has placed such power? Is it only the atoms and the electrons that have such tremendous energy? Are we to believe that God has left man—the master-piece of His creation—powerless?

Not if we believe, as we do, that man is made in the image of God, that he was created to have dominion over the earth. The question is: What kind of power are we talking about? If it's power to master nature we're talking about, then man has that power. Already he has hit the moon and is preparing for space travel. But if it's power to master himself we're talking about, then it's an altogether different story. Sir Charles Darwin, grandson of the great evolutionist, writes, "Man can now aspire to the complete mastery of nature, but subject to the one condition that he can master himself."

It is this power to master himself that man lacks. Evidence of this is how depressingly easy it is to find people today who know how to say, "I can't . . . I can't control my temper . . . I can't resist temptation . . I can't live a pure life in today's so-ciety . . I can't come to church every Sunday . . . I can't pray . . . I can't be a victorious Christian . . . I can't . . . I can't . . . I can't."

Where does one receive the strength to overcome this in-adequacy, this powerlessness? There is no other way than by attaching ourselves to Someone who is all-powerful: God in the Person of Christ.

A father stood watching as his son tried in vain to move a rock. He tried and tried, but was unable to budge it. "Son, are you sure you're using all your strength?" asked the father. "Of course, I am," said the boy. "But you haven't asked me to help," said the father.

How often do we try to remove from our lives some sin or passion that has enslaved us. We try and try, but in vain; for we rely solely on our own meager strength. We forget that we have a heavenly Father who is all-powerful, who is willing to come to our assistance with tremendous power, who stands just waiting for us to ask Him for this supernatural help, who "is able," writes St. Paul, "to supply all your needs according to his riches in glory in Christ Jesus."

One of Aesop's fables tells of a lion which had taken on

more than it had calculated in attacking a fierce, wild bull. The lion then called on its friend, the dolphin, to help. Immediately the dolphin raced to its rescue. But once he was out of water the dolphin was as helpless as any fish could be. His piteous cries only added to his friend's predicament. Aesop intended the moral to be this: "When you need help, be sure to ask someone who is not only *willing*, but also *able* to give it."

The God in whom we believe is not only willing but able. Listen to what various people in the New Testament say about the Lord Jesus' ability:

"He is *able* to help them that are tempted."

"He is *able* to keep you from falling."

"He is *able* to supply all your need."

"He is *able* to do exceeding abundantly above all that we ask or think."

"He is *able* to save to the uttermost."

"He is *able* to subdue all things unto Himself."

"I can do *all things* through Christ who strengtheneth me."

"We are *more than* conquerors through Him who loved us."

This is not just talk. This is the actual clinical experience of people who have discovered Christ's power in their lives.

When a certain miner was converted to Christianity, he testified, "I was a bad lot; I drank; I pawned the furniture; I knocked my wife about; but now life is real living, and splendidly worthwhile." Asked how his fellow miners reacted to his conversion, he said, "Today they asked me, 'You don't really believe that old yarn about Jesus turning the water into wine?' And I told them, 'I know nothing about water and wine, but I know this, that in my house Christ has turned beer into furniture; and that is a good enough miracle for me.' "

We believe in a God who is *able*. ABLE to conquer sin. ABLE to impart new life. ABLE to pick up the pieces of a broken life and make it whole again. He is ABLE to do this, if we will let Him, if we will repent and seek His forgiveness.

How can we receive this divine power to master ourselves? There is only one way: by attaching ourselves to our Lord Jesus Christ, who is able, who is all-powerful. How do we attach ourselves to Christ?

By PRAYER. There is power in prayer. Moses prayed.

The sea was divided. Elijah prayed. Rain descended upon a parched earth. Daniel prayed. The lions were muzzled. Paul and Silas prayed. The prison doors were opened. Jesus prayed in Gethsemane. An angel appeared to strengthen Him. There is power in prayer.

There is power in the Word of God. Augustine read it and was converted. Others read it, and found it to be the door to a new life. Still others have read it, and have found power for daily living. "God's Word has hands and feet," someone has written. "It runs after a man; it grips him. Let it loose and things will happen."

There is power in prayer. There is power in the Word of God. But by far the greatest source of power for the Christian is the Sacrament of Holy Communion. "Truly, truly, I say to you, unless you eat the flesh of the Son of man and drink his blood, you have no life in you; he who eats my flesh and drinks my blood has eternal life, and I will raise him up at the last day. For my flesh is food indeed, and my blood is drink indeed. He who eats my flesh and drinks my blood abides in me, and I in him" (John 6:53–56). Here is power. Here is strength. Here is energy compared to which the energy in the atom pales into insignificance.

We receive within us the all-powerful God. We receive within us Him "who is able to supply all our need." We receive within us, writes St. Chrysostom, the same body of our Lord that was born in the manger of Bethlehem, the same body that walked on the Sea of Galilee, the same body that was crucified on Calvary, the same body that was resurrected from the tomb, the same body that ascended into heaven and now sits on the right hand of God the Father. There is no power in life greater than this.

Nebuchadnezzar came running to the lions' den after a sleepless night and asked: "Daniel, was your God able?" From experience Daniel could say, "My God is able."

Able to do what?

Able to help us do the good that we don't always even want to do.

Able to give courage and insight for the day's needs.

Able to forgive our helplessness, our lack of faith, and all
the sins and shortcomings that plague our lives.

Able to give whatever we most need, "above what we ask
or think," as Paul says.

Able to overcome our fears and hopelessness.

"Now unto *him that is able to keep* you from falling, and
to present you faultless before the presence of his glory with
exceeding joy; to the only wise God our Saviour, be glory
and majesty, dominion and power, both now and ever" (Jude
24, 25).

Chapter Twelve

WORDS! WORDS! WORDS!

POLONIUS ASKED HAMLET what he was reading. His reply was, "Words, words, words." Only words! And yet how great is the power of words!

The Apostle Paul asks, "Does a fountain send forth at the same place sweet water and bitter?" No fountain can do that, except one, and that is the fountain of the tongue, with which men bless God and curse people who are made in the image of God.

"Word, words, words." Mere words! Words are as common as blossoms on a spring day; yet how mysterious their spell, how mighty their power, and how irrevocable their influence. Words are the transcript of man's mind, the index of his character. "Thy speech betrayeth thee." Homer used to speak of "winged" words, and his words still wing their way in the firmament of human thought long centuries after they first commenced their flight.

A well-known publisher says, "If you are an articulate person, you utter some 30,000 words each day." He might have added that we utter many of them without thought of consideration, little realizing that every word we speak either curses or blesses, and can never be recalled.

A peasant once slandered a friend, only to find that what he had said was not true. Troubled in his conscience, he went to a monk to seek advice. The monk said to him, "If you want to make peace with your conscience, you must fill a bag with feathers and go to every doorstep in the village and drop on each of them one feather." The peasant did as he was told. He thought he had completed the penance for his sin. "Not yet!" said the monk sternly. "Take up your bag, go the rounds again, and gather up every feather you have dropped." "But the wind has blown them all away by this time!" exclaimed the peasant. "Yes, my son," answered the monk, "and so it is with gossip and slander. Words are easily dropped, but no matter how hard you try, you never can get them back again."

As children we used to say, "Sticks and stones may break my bones, but names can never hurt me." But now as adults we know that this simply isn't true. For the wounds in the body made by stones may heal, but the hurt in the heart made by unkind and careless words may endure for a lifetime.

Our Lord not only pronounced a judgment upon words, but He gave the reason for our accountability as to the words we speak. The reason is that words tell the secret of the heart. A French cynic and diplomat said that words were intended to conceal thought. However that may be in diplomacy, it is not true in life. *Words reveal thought and uncover the heart.* "Out of the abundance of the heart the mouth speaks. The good man out of his good treasure brings forth good things, and the evil man out of his evil treasure brings forth evil things." "Therefore," says Christ, "every idle word that men shall speak, they shall give account thereof in the day of judgement." "Words, words, words!" Only words. Yet it is by our words that we are known and shall be judged.

To regulate the tongue it is necessary to keep the heart pure. For "the tongue's great storehouse is the heart." If one carrying a bucket of water is accidentally bumped or jostled by someone else, he spills water; for he can spill only what is in the bucket. Amid the jostling of life, we can spill out of the lips only what is in the heart.

The heart of man, his mind, his tongue, his whole being must be controlled by the love of Christ. Many times we are not as Christian as we suppose. There remain areas in our lives that have never been brought under the purifying and controlling love of Christ. "If any one thinks he is religious," says the Bible, "and does not bridle his tongue . . . this man's religion is in vain" (James 1:26).

Think for a moment of the far-reaching influence the words of parents have on their children. The mother who tells her weeping daughter on the day after her father's death: "Your father died because you were not a good girl." These words become imbedded in the girl's soul and she will go through life with the horribly oppressive guilt feeling that she caused her father's death—a guilt feeling that will torment her every day of her life and may lead to mental illness. "Words!" Only words! Yet how destructive!

Consider on the other hand what effect one kind word of praise can have. When Arthur Compton, who has been called "one of the immortals of science," was ten years old he wrote an essay taking issue with experts on why some elephants were three-toed and others five-toed. He brought it to his mother to read. The mother had a hard time to keep from laughing, but she knew how seriously her son took his ideas so she sat down and worked on them with him. Later he told her, "If you had laughed at me that day, I think you would have killed my interest in scientific research." *One word of praise!* How far it went in creating one of the truly great scientists of this world!

Consider how important words are in marriage. A wife, sitting in the presence of a marriage counselor, says, "We have been married over twenty years, and I do not think he has told me once in these years that he loves me." Her husband answers, "She knows I love her." The marriage counselor, turning to the woman, says, "Do you think he loves you?" "Yes, I think he does but he never tells me." Whereupon the husband stubbornly insisted, "She knows I love her." Think of what one word of love, spoken daily, would have meant to that marriage.

Consider the importance of words in human relations. People are almost exactly what we expect them to be, because they try so hard to live up to the image we have of them. Try this some time. Say to someone, "I believe you are a very friendly and understanding person." Even though he may have shown tendencies to be just the opposite kind of person, he may go all out in order to prove that you are right.

"Words, words, words," said Hamlet. Only words. Yet how great in power!

May we live ever in closer and closer fellowship with our Lord Jesus that our tongue may be the tongue of Christ speaking words of purity and truth, of encouragement and hope, of faith and love, words that endure forever and which will echo sweetly for us on the day of Judgment. The world today needs much love, much understanding, and much kindness. We can bring these healing powers to the world through the wonder of words. They are the gift of God. Let us treasure them and treat them as winged angels of beauty, truth and goodness.

Chapter Thirteen

"REMEMBER
WHAT YOUR FATHERS DID"

SOME TIME AGO A FATHER took his fourteen-year-old son to see Omaha Beach. He wanted him to see where once he had stood between life and death. Then he had been a lieutenant colonel with the Rangers of the United States Army. As he and his boy stood on the naked beach of France, everything became vivid in his mind. He recalled the scaling of the walls; he experienced again the fierce combat; he remembered the horrors of war. Everything he touched—a rotting piece of rope, an iron hook, a rusty chain, a broken tree—came back to life. It stood for something. Like the warriors of Joshua's time, he wanted to say to his son, "Remember what your fathers did."

The Sunday before Pentecost is called on our church calendar the Sunday of the Holy Fathers. On this day each year the Orthodox Church calls on us to remember what our fathers did: specifically the 318 Church Fathers who came together in 325 A.D. in Nicea to form the First Ecumenical Council. The Emperor Constantine had just put an end to the bloody, three-hundred-year persecution of the Church, during which eleven million Christians gave their lives for Christ. Christians now began coming out of the catacombs to worship in churches. In Dorner's words, "The ekklesia martyrousa" became "the ekklesia theologousa," i.e., the Church of the martyrs now became the Church of the theologians. These 318 bishops came together to define the teachings of Christ which were being challenged by false teachers. They gave us, as a result, among other things, the Nicene Creed, the summary of our faith, which is still read in the liturgy every Sunday. In the remaining six ecumenical councils which met over a five-hundred-year period the Church Fathers gave the Christian world some of the finest definitions of the Godhead and the Trinity ever devised.

The Orthodox Church is often called the Church of the

Fathers because she maintains a living connection with these early Church Fathers. We are not a Church that was instituted a few years ago, or even a few centuries ago. The early Fathers are part of our church history. In fact our Church came to be called Orthodox, meaning true faith, because of the great emphasis the early Fathers of the Greek Church placed upon preserving the true faith of Christ. As Orthodox Christians, we have inherited all the experience of 19 centuries of Christian living and thinking and believing. We have behind us hundreds of believing men and women of every tribe and tongue, witnessing to the truth of the Gospel, often dying for it in order to hand it down to us.

That is why when we Orthodox Christians pick up the Bible to read it, we do not act as if these 19 centuries of church history did not exist. We read the Bible and we gain a better understanding of it because we consider how the Holy Spirit has guided the Church Fathers in the past to interpret certain difficult passages in Scripture. This is what we mean by Sacred Tradition. We do not mean, as Dr. Florovsky emphasizes, the traditions of men or a slavish attachment to the past. By Sacred Tradition we mean A LIVING CONNECTION WITH THE ENTIRE PAST EXPERIENCE OF THE CHURCH, nineteen centuries of it during which the Holy Spirit has been acting and speaking through the Church.

There is a great sense of community in the Orthodox Church. Orthodox Christians never pray alone. We pray together with all the saints who have passed on. We pray not as individuals but as members of the body of Christ, i.e., the Church. We pray with the Theotokos, the apostles, the angels, the martyrs and the saints of all ages. They are present at every liturgy as depicted in the iconography of our Church. Around the figure of Christ in the dome are gathered the angels, apostles, saints and martyrs on the walls. All these constitute the Church Triumphant in heaven. Then we, the congregation, on the ground-floor of the Church, represent the Church Militant on earth. Thus around the figure of Christ in the dome is gathered for every liturgy the entire Church, both that in heaven and that on earth.

Dr. Howard Rome, psychiatrist at the Mayo Clinic, said

once that when he sits with a patient in a room, he considers that he is not alone with the patient. Behind the patient, he says, stand, like a Greek chorus, all the people with whom the patient has ever lived. They are all in the room with him, for they have left their indelible mark on this patient's personality either for good or ill.

The Orthodox Church seeks to remind us that we Christians do not stand alone. Behind us stands a cloud of witnesses. Behind us, for example, stand those 318 Church Fathers who came to the First Ecumenical Council. They came, bearing the scars of martyrdom, some with one eye and some with one arm. Some without legs and some with disfigured faces. They came with twisted and paralyzed limbs. They came from all over the Empire to bear witness with their whole personality to the truth they believed: that Jesus Christ is Lord.

These martyrs stand behind us. And behind them stand others: Peter and James and Stephen and Ignatius and Polycarp and Paul and Athanasius and Chrysostom—a whole army of noble martyrs who rejoiced that they were counted worthy to suffer for the name of Christ.

When the 1964 Olympic Games opened in Tokyo, the Olympic Flame was brought by plane from Athens, Greece, the site of the first Olympics in 776 B.C. From the plane the burning torch was carried by relays of runners, who passed the flame from one to the next until it reached the site of the games. It linked the Olympic Games in Tokyo with their source in the past.

As Christians we are all "torch bearers." We have received the light of life from its source in God. The torch was handed to us by a great line of believers stretching back to Christ himself—apostles, martyrs, saints. It is our privilege and duty to pass it on to others.

Einstein said once, "A hundred times every day I remind myself that my inner and outer life depend on the labors of other men, living and dead. I must exert myself in order to give in the measure as I have received and am still receiving." Think of those 318 blind, crippled Church Fathers meeting in Nicea in 325 A.D. to pass on to us the lighted torch of Christ.

Think of what they suffered to place the torch in our hands today.

Violinist Jascha Heifetz has virtually retired from the concert stage to devote his talents to teaching. Explaining why he did this, he said: "I should like to pass on what I know to my pupils. To be an artist is like being entrusted with something precious for a brief time. It is the duty of an artist to hand it on, like those Greek runners who passed on the lighted torch, one to another."

We are all entrusted for a brief time with something precious—the Lord Jesus Christ "in whom are hid all the treasures of wisdom and knowledge" and, as the Gospel says, "whom to know is life eternal." This is the lighted torch we are to pass on to our children and to our friends who do not know Christ.

Dr. Ralph Sockman tells of watching the 1948 Olympic Games in London. A relay race was on. The French team had started well. But as the torch was being passed to the third runner he dropped it. The accident put the team out of the running. The runner threw himself on the ground, flung his hands to his head in a gesture of despair and openly wept. His emotional outburst continued as he was led from the area.

To take defeat so tearfully might seem a bit unsportsmanlike. But one should remember how many persons were involved in that runner's failure. There were his watching compatriots, whose hopes were dashed. There were the teammates who had run before him and whose work was ruined by his blunder. And then there were the runners who were to come after but who never got the chance to run because of the accident.

The whole spectacle made Dr. Sockman realize how much life was like a relay race. In the race of life, no one starts from scratch. Others have run the race before us. Still others wait to run the race after us. If we fail to pass on the lighted torch they have given us, we fail not only them but we also deprive countless others in the future of the light of Christ.

William L. Stidger told the story of a rugged mountaineer in Tennessee. The government was building a lake to generate electrical power. Many homes had to be moved. But one man stubbornly refused to move out of his home. They argued with this man and even built him another home not far away which was much nicer. Still he refused to move.

They kept asking him why he would not move. Finally he explained that his grandfather had started a fire on the hearth in the old cabin and instructed his son to keep the fire going always as a sacred family symbol. His father had kept the fire going and, before he died, he transmitted the heritage to his son. The man said, "I must keep alive the fires of my fathers."

So the engineers carefully gathered up the fire from the old hearth and carried it, still burning, to the new home. Then the man was satisfied to move.

Every year on the Sunday of the Holy Fathers the Orthodox Church calls on us to remember those who stand behind us. Remember the Church Fathers. Remember the apostles, the martyrs, the saints. Remember what they suffered to place the lighted torch of Christ in our hands. Remember to keep it burning brightly. Remember to pass it on to others that "the world may see your good works and glorify your Father who is in heaven."

Chapter Fourteen

"STIR UP WHAT YOU HAVE"

DURING THE SECOND WORLD WAR there was a great shortage of sugar. A man seated at a restaurant counter complained to the waitress about the small amount of sugar in his coffee. The waitress glared at him for a moment and then said: "Stir up what you've got!"

The tragedy in life is not that we have not been given talents and capabilities by God. The tragedy is that we have not been stirring. We have not been using what God has given us. All of us carry on below our maximum. Few of us achieve our potential in life. Few of us become fully what God has endowed us to become—mainly because we fail to stir up what we have.

Some time ago there was a remarkable play entitled "Sunrise at Campobello." The play opens just as Franklin D. Roosevelt returns from a swim in the cold waters off the coast of Nova Scotia, where his summer home was located. During the hours of that night he was stricken ill and was paralyzed to such an extent that he was practically helpless. His mother wanted him to return to Hyde Park and be an invalid for the rest of his life; to be waited on by servants; to retire from the ordinary demands of his life completely; but one of his friends pled with him not to do it, but rather to make every possible effort to get back on his feet and resume his place in society, making full use of his talents. Occasionally, when everyone else had left the room, sitting there in his wheelchair, he made the effort to get out of the chair and onto his feet without assistance, only to fall flat on his face, then crawl back onto the chair and try it again. At other times he got down on the floor and crawled from one chair to the next, trying to exercise his muscles and regain some of his strength. Finally, he did get back on his feet, and went on to become president of this great country for twelve long years.

In the face of tremendous odds, he did not fail to develop what little life he had left in his legs. He did not sit back and feel sorry for himself. Instead he stirred up what little strength he had and it grew.

One day an admirer asked the great pianist Paderewski: "Is it true that you still practice every day?"

"Yes," said the pianist, "I practice at least eight hours every day."

"You must have a world of patience," said the other.

"I have no more patience than the next fellow," said Paderewski. "I just use mine." He stirred up what he had.

In the Gospels we read of two blind men who came to Jesus and cried, "Have mercy on us, Son of David." Jesus said to them, "Do you believe that I am able to do this?" They said to Him, "Yes, Lord." Then He touched their eyes, saying, "According to your faith, be it done to you." And their eyes were opened. After reading this story some may say, "If only we had such a faith, a faith that would bring us to Jesus with every one of our burdens, knowing that He cares, knowing that He will stand by our side and help us carry our heaviest burdens as He did the two blind men, if only we had such a faith." You can have such a faith if only you will stir up the little faith you already have. Feed it with prayer. Nourish it with daily readings from the Word of God. Strengthen it with weekly attendance at the divine liturgy. Reinforce it frequently with the Sacrament of Holy Communion. Stir up what faith you have and watch how it will grow!

There are those who complain that they cannot live a Christ-like life. "I simply don't have the strength," they say. To these voices our Lord would say, "Stir up what strength you have, however small it may be." It is only when we ourselves are willing to resist sin and evil with whatever feeble strength we have that the Lord will add His strength to ours and help us overcome defeat.

It is not that others have more strength, more patience, more faith, than we have. It is that they stir up what they have and it grows. It grows by God's grace and enables us to be "more than conquerors through him who loved us."

Chapter Fifteen

PRIDE AND HUMILITY

A YOUNG GIRL IN ENGLAND was applying for a position as a housemaid. She showed her recommendations to a prospective employer. After reading them, the woman said to the applicant, "You certainly have some fine recommendations here." The girl replied, much pleased, "I am glad you like them. I wrote them myself."

The Pharisee did the same. He took a census of his virtues and showed his self-written recommendations to God. He prayed, "God, I thank thee that I am not like other men, extortioners, unjust, adulterers, or even like this tax collector. I fast twice a week, I give tithes of all that I get." The Pharisee reminds one of the Hollywood actor who said once, "'I used to be quite conceited. But my psychiatrist cured me of that, and now I am one of the nicest guys in town." His sin was the sin of pride.

But what's wrong with pride? some will ask. Isn't pride a natural good? Without pride we would be doormats. We would not develop our talents. We would feel inadequate and inferior. Without pride we wouldn't wash our faces, tidy ourselves in any way, take satisfaction in our work, or keep ourselves fit for our highest achievements. Without pride we would sag as personalities. There is a healthy pride which a man needs to have in order to function as a person.

If pride has been called the greatest of all sins, it is because it closes the door to God and other people. It builds barriers between man and God, between man and man. It says, "I don't need you. I am self-sufficient." If sincere humility, on the other hand, has been called the greatest of all virtues, it is because it keeps the door open to God and other people. It tears down barriers.

Consider how much pride there is in some of our prayers. A woman said once that she had lost her faith in God because

He did not answer her prayers as she thought they should have been answered. To feel that God must do everything according to our wisdom is pride at its highest level. True prayer is humble. It leaves room for God's wisdom and love. It says, "Thy will be done, O Lord."

Consider how much pride is involved in our racial difficulties today. The Pharisee, who brags about being better than others, is not confined to the time of Jesus. He lives today. He takes pride in the color of his skin. He looks down on others who have a darker skin than his own. The Pharisee of race prays even today, "God, I thank Thee that I am not like other men. . . ."

Consider the pride we take in our positions.

The conductor of a famous symphony orchestra was asked which instrument was the most difficult to play. He thought for a moment and then said, "Second fiddle. I can get plenty of first violinists. But to find one who can play second fiddle with enthusiasm—that's the problem. And if we have no second fiddle, we have no harmony."

Consider Jesus who had the highest position in the universe. If anyone should have been proud of his position, He should have been. Yet, says Archbishop Wm. Temple, "In a moment when He was especially conscious of His divine mission and authority, knowing that He came forth from God and went unto God, what did He do? Did He sit on a throne and ask His disciples to bow before Him in homage? No! He took a towel and performed the task of the lowest slave, the task that no one else wished to perform. He washed His disciples' feet. That is what He thought it was like to be God." He showed us that He who occupies the greatest position in life is not he who sits on a throne but he who serves.

Consider next how pride in our own goodness keeps us from receiving God's forgiveness. Jesus said once, "I did not come to invite the righteous but sinners to repentance." What He was really saying is this, "I did not come to invite people who are so self-satisfied, so convinced of their own goodness that they don't need anyone's help; I came to invite people who are very conscious of their sin and desperately aware of their need for a saviour." He was saying, "It is only those who know how much they need me who can accept my invitation." The Pharisee was convinced of his own goodness. His cup was too full of self. There was no room for God. But the Publican was aware of his sinfulness. He emptied his cup of sin and self. He prayed, "God, be merciful to me a sinner." And God filled his cup with forgiveness.

Consider finally how pride in our own strength keeps us from receiving God's power. An alcoholic must sacrifice his pride completely before he can be cured. He must acknowledge that he cannot overcome drinking on his own. He must admit his own inadequacy and call upon God for strength. And yet this is one of the most difficult things for the alcoholic to do. Why? Because of his pride. He likes to fool himself into thinking that he can quit whenever he wants, when the truth is that he cannot.

A man turned on the hose once to water his garden, but no water came forth. He called out to his son to check the spigot to see what was wrong. The son brought it to his father's attention that the reason there was no water was that his foot was on the hose. The father stepped off the hose and the water immediately poured forth. So it is with us many times. If we are not victorious Christians it is because SELF stands in the way. "I can do this on my own. I don't need God's help," says the proud person. But the humble person keeps SELF out of the way and his life is filled with strength from God.

It was brought to the attention of one of the popes once that a certain abbess was performing miracles in a convent. The Pope sent St. Philip Neri to investigate. After a long trip he arrived there, tired and exhausted. He took off his shoes which were loaded with mud and asked the abbess to clean them for him. The abbess stuck up her nose haughtily and walked away. St. Philip Neri left the convent and returning to the Pope, he reported, "There are no miracles performed in that convent. Where there is no humility there can be no miracles."

If there *are* miracles where there is humility, it is because humility helps us realize our sins and weaknesses—our emptiness—and keeps the door open always to God's love, forgiveness and power.

Chapter Sixteen

THE GREAT BRIDGE BUILDER

A GREAT AND BELOVED BRITISH PREACHER, Richard Sheppard, was visiting some troops during the war. The military chaplain pointed to one soldier and said to Dr. Sheppard, "I can't get near him at all. Religion does not interest him." Dr. Sheppard walked up to the soldier and struck up a lively conversation. The two seemed to have an enjoyable time together. The military chaplain was astonished. "I should be glad, Dr. Sheppard," he said later, "if you would explain what religious approach you make to a person who seems entirely indifferent to religion." "Religion," said Dr. Sheppard, "I didn't talk religion at all. I told him two funny stories and then inquired about his mother."

The chaplain learned a great lesson that day from a great preacher. He learned that good humor, good will and caring are great bridge builders between people. Only after such a bridge is built between two persons can the traffic of something more intimate, like religion, pass.

The greatest bridge builder of all is our Lord, Jesus Christ, one of whose titles is, PONTIFEX MAXIMUS: The Supreme Bridge Builder. He built the bridge which spans the "widest chasm" and the "longest span" known to man—the span from God to man, from sin to forgiveness, from separation to closeness with God, from death to life eternal. "No man comes to the Father except through me," He said.

A great example of how Christ built bridges between himself and other people is the Samaritan woman. When Jesus met her at the well, He did something which no other Jew of His day would have done. He spoke to her. In those days it was unheard of for a man, especially a rabbi, to speak to a woman in public, especially to a Samaritan woman, for the Jews and the Samaritans despised each other, and even more especially to a woman of ill repute. Yet Jesus spoke to her. He spoke not to moralize or condemn her. He spoke not to degrade her. He spoke not to say, "You are a sinner. You need to be saved and only I can save you." No! Rather, He spoke to say, "Give me a drink." By asking her for a drink, He made her feel needed; He made her feel important; He built up her self-respect and dignity. So Jesus began by building a bridge between himself and the Samaritan woman. Over this bridge He was able to approach her later on the serious issues of the water of life and the salvation of her soul.

"Bridge building," someone has said, "is the chief unfinished task of human relations today." What we need today are more bridges—usable bridges between parents and children, negroes and whites, God and man.

Consider the gap that exists today between parents and children. Young people complain that parents do not understand them, that there is no communication between them and their parents no matter what the subject under consideration is—school, job, friends or morals. Parents, they complain, will not listen. They never hear them out. They brush all explanations aside. As one young man put it, "The conversation at our house is more like an inquisition. Father talks more like a prosecuting attorney than an understanding parent. Our parents demand much, criticize much, censure much. They simply do not understand us."

Surveys show that young people want to come to their parents with their problems. But they can't. They can't because the bridge between them has been torn down. One of our greatest tasks, as parents today, is to re-build this bridge between us and our children. We can re-build it by listening to our children when they speak, by acting not as prosecuting attorneys, but as loving parents, by understanding that our children are still children, and not always censuring them for their immaturities, by being available to them, by leaving some of our own interests as adults, and entering into some of the interests of our young people, by family prayer, by having more activities in the home that will bring the whole family together. There are many great and famous bridges in the world that span great distances, but one of the greatest bridges is the one we parents can build in the home to span the distance between us and our children.

Next, consider the gap that exists today between the races in this country. Too long have we denied the Negro his God-given rights; too long have we refused to accept the fact that he, too, is created in the image of God and is equal to us in every respect; too long have we used him as a slave, as a tool, to enrich our economy; too long have we denied him jobs and exiled him to a ghetto of utter poverty.

As Dr. Martin Luther King wrote in his now famous "Letter from a Birmingham Jail":

"I guess it is easy for those who have never felt the stinging facts of segregation to say, 'Wait!' But when you have seen vicious mobs lynch your mothers and fathers at will and drown your sisters and brothers at whim; when you have seen hate-filled policemen curse, kick, brutalize and even kill your black brothers and sisters with impunity . . . when you suddenly find your tongue twisted and your speech stammering as you seek to explain to your six-year-old daughter why she can't go to the public amusement park that has been advertised on television, and see tears welling up in her eyes when she is told that Funtown is closed to colored children . . . when you take a cross-country drive and find it necessary to sleep night after night in the uncomfortable quarters of your automobile because no motel will accept you . . . when you are forever fighting a degenerating sense of 'nobodyness'; then you will understand why we find it difficult to wait. There comes a time when the cup of endurance runs over, and men are no longer willing to be plunged into an abyss of injustice where they experience the bleakness of corroding despair."

It is time we repented of this, our great sin, and cried out to God for forgiveness for treating our fellow man so shamefully. It is time we tried to atone for our great sin by building bridges of understanding and love between the races, by becoming involved in civil rights, by doing what we can to open doors to Negroes: doors of education, doors of employment, doors of adequate housing.

Finally, there is the great bridge between man and God established by Christ. Sometimes it is not a well travelled bridge. Sometimes, as far as some of us are concerned, it is a bridge that no longer exists. This happens especially when we sin. For sin separates; it creates distance between man and God. We feel far from God. We feel that God is angry with us, that He wants to punish us. We are haunted by guilt. We run from God. Yet the truth of the matter is that even though we may be running from God, God is not running from us. He stands beside us even in our sin, inviting us to come back.

A story is told of a young girl who wandered away from God and her parents' home. She went deeply into sin. One night, in a wild frenzy, she concluded that she would commit suicide. But before doing so, she decided to look once more at the home where she was born and had spent her youth. In the middle of the night she came to her mother's cottage. She saw, to her surprise, that the front door was wide open. In fear lest some harm might have come to her old mother, she called out to her. The old mother got up, came down and said, "Janey, it is many a long day since you left home, but always the prayer has been in my heart, 'Lord, send her home.' And I said, 'Whether she comes by day or night, I want her to see an open door and know she is welcome.' " The weeping girl fell into the arms of love and forgiveness.

The door of Christ's heart is always open to receive us if we will come back to Him. He is the great bridge builder. He can bridge the distance between every sinner and God if we will repent of our sins and accept His forgiveness. He can bridge the wide expanse of inner emptiness with God's love. He can bridge the great chasm of loneliness with the presence of God. He can bridge the painful gap of guilt and despair with God's peace and joy. Christ can be such a bridge builder for you!

A little girl, not used to traveling, was making a train trip across the country with her mother. Looking out the train window, she could see rivers and streams ahead. She worried how the train would be able to cross those bodies of water.

As they drew near the river for the first time, the little girl saw the bridge which was to provide the way over. Two or three times the same thing happened. Finally, the little girl leaned back in the train seat and with a long sigh of relief and confidence said, "Somebody has been here before us and built bridges for us all the way."

Christ has been here before us and He has built bridges for us all the way—the bridge from sin to forgiveness, from despair to hope, from doubt to faith, from death to life. And He expects us, His followers, to be bridge builders as we pass through this world, building bridges of understanding and love between us and our fellow man.

Chapter Seventeen

WHAT'S PLAYING IN YOUR LIFE?

WHEN WE GO TO THE MOVIES we ask: "What's playing?" Few of us ever ask the other more important question: "What's playing in my life? Who is the producer? Who or what is playing the chief role?"

There are those who say that they are what they are because of their *environment*. It was the theory of the French philosopher, Rousseau, that the evil that is done in the world is due to evil surroundings and environment. But the deeper question is: Who created that environment? What is environment but the result of the free choices of other people? And in most cases do we not choose cr create our own environment? No one would advise a young man or woman to place himself deliberately in an evil environment, but the truth is that high Christian character can be developed in spite of bad environment. Adam and Eve lived in the perfect environment, Paradise, and still they sinned. Lot, on the other hand, lived in the most wicked environment, Sodom and Gommorah, yet he remained righteous. John and Judas had exactly the same environment, but one fell, the other rose to sainthood. Environment *conditions* character but it does not *cause* it.

There are those who say that they are what they are because of *circumstances*. We have a very familiar phrase which, I think, is very suggestive. We say, "Under the circumstances." But why should we be *under* the circumstances? Why not rise *above* them? Why be slaves and not masters? Under the circumstances Abraham Lincoln, whose life was one failure after another, should never have become president. But he did not remain *under* the circumstances. He rose above them. Circumstances make a man only in the sense that he permits them to make him.

There are those who say that they are what they are because of *heredity*. They like to blame their ancestors for their ills, their weaknesses, their faults, their sins. And their ancestors—poor souls—are no longer present to defend themselves. A restless woman who acted rather compulsively, seeking to explain herself, said, "I myself am really not that way. I guess I owe that to my ancestors." Of course, her ancestors were not wholly without blame. But there are things for which we, not our ancestors, are to blame. We cannot put all the blame on heredity. In a way, life is like playing a game of cards. We have been dealt a certain hand; we have been given certain limitations through heredity. But it's up to us to play as best we can with the cards we have without constantly using our ancestors as scapegoats for our inability to play the game well.

There are those who say that they are what they are because of the way they were treated in *childhood*. True, childhood experiences have great influence in a person's life. But we were never meant by God to be enslaved by childhood experiences. By God's grace we can rise above them. We don't have to remain children all our lives. We don't have to go through life saying, "I am what I am because my parents mistreated me in childhood and I can never change." We can rise above childhood experiences. We can master them. We can overcome them. Your parents may not have treated you well in childhood, but how are you treating yourself now? Are you wallowing in self-pity or are you forging ahead trying with God's grace to overcome the limitations of childhood?

Finally there are those who say that they are what they are because of *God*. "God made me this way," they say. "I can't help it." They act as if they were puppets with God pulling the strings, as if they had no free will to choose their own destiny. There was a minister once who believed in predestination. He believed that we are what we are because of God, that God decides before we are born what we shall be and what we shall do. One day this minister was to exchange pulpits with another clergyman. The other minister, Lyman Beecher, did not believe in predestination.

On Sunday the two clergymen met on their way to each other's church. The minister who believed that God decides

our destiny said, "Dr. Beecher, I wish to call to your attention that before the creation of the world God arranged that
you were to preach in my pulpit and I in yours on this particular Sabbath." "Is that so?" said Beecher. "Then I won't
do it!" And, turning his horse, he returned to his church. It
is not God who pulls the strings; it is not God who decides
our destiny; we have been given the great gift of free will
by God to decide our own destiny, to pull our own strings. We
are what we are not because of God but because of our own
free will, our own free decisions in life.

We are not, then, reeds blown about by the winds of environment, circumstance, heredity, childhood, or even God.
We are *more than conquerors* through him that loved us."
Man was never meant by God to be a slave to his environment
or to anything else. He was created to rise above his limitations.
Consider, for a moment, the problems man encounters today
in outer space. So hostile to man is the environment of outer
space that without pressurized suits man's blood would bub-
ble and boil, his bodily tissues would burst, and blazing light
from a brilliant sun in a black sky would severely injure his
eyes. Our lives would quickly come to an end. Yet, just as man
through science is rapidly overcoming the extremely hostile
environment of outer space, so, with God's grace, he can
overcome a hostile moral environment and rise above it.

We are tempted many times to project on others the blame
for our sins. "I am not responsible for this sin," many will
rationalize. "It's my biological or emotional makeup that's
to blame." But is it really our environment? Is it really circumstances or heredity or childhood that make us this way? Or is
it our refusal to rise above these limitations with God's help?
Is it really I, Lord? Is it I?

As children of God, created in His own image, we are free
to choose; we are free to choose to go either our own selfish
way or God's way; we are free to choose either heaven or hell;
we are responsible beings. This is why we shall all be called
upon one day to give an account of ourselves to God.

The direction of your life depends not so much on circumstances as it does on the goal you choose for yourself. For
a person chooses his environment in accordance with the goal

he has chosen. Some choose to live always in an atmosphere of greed; it dominates their whole life. Others choose to live in an atmosphere of sex. Still others choose to live in an atmosphere of failure and defeat, of petty gossip and grumbling, of negative thinking and chronic unhappiness. And some, thank God, choose to live in Christ and for Christ, in an environment of faith, prayer and love, an environment of unbreakable good will and inviolable peace.

In which environment have you chosen to live? Who or what is playing in your life? Are you a reed blown about aimlessly by the wind of circumstance? Or are you a sailboat with your sail set, letting the winds of life guide you in the direction Christ points out to you, the direction that leads to forgiveness, to peace, to life eternal?

"Who shall separate us from the love of Christ?" asks St. Paul. Then he draws up a list of circumstances: "Shall tribulation, or distress, or persecution, or famine, or nakedness, or peril, or sword? . . . No, in all these things [or circumstances] we are more than conquerors through him who loved us" (Rom. 8:35-37).

Chapter Eighteen

THEN WHAT?

A CERTAIN MAN asked a high school student: "What are
you going to do when you finish high school?"

"I am going to college."

"Then what?"

"Then I would like to become a successful attorney."

"Then what?"

"Then I will purchase a fine home in the suburbs and raise
a family."

"Then what?"

"Then I hope I can become a judge some day."

"Then what?"

"Then I'd like to take a trip around the world."

"Then what?"

"Then I suppose some day I will eventually die like everyone else."

"Then what?"

"Well, I hadn't thought much about what comes after
death," said the student.

St. Paul had thought about what comes after death. He
writes in II Timothy 4:7, 8, "The time of my departure
has come. I have fought the good fight. I have finished the
race. I have kept the faith. Henceforth there is laid up for
me the crown of righteousness, which the Lord, the righteous judge, will award me on that Day, and not only to me
but also to all who have loved his appearing."

A passenger asked a sailor once how far the "Queen Mary"
would have to go before she could stop if she were going full
speed. "Well," answered the sailor, "She couldn't even slow
down in less than a mile. You see, with a big ship like the
'Queen Mary,' *you have to think a mile ahead.*"

Most of the tragedies of life occur because we do not think

ahead. We consider the present with no thought of the future. It is good to ask ourselves the question, "Then what?" The students of the great Greek philosopher Socrates met every answer with another question: "If this is true, then what?"

I give food to the hungry, water to the thirsty, a welcome to a stranger, clothes to the needy, THEN WHAT? Then, says Jesus, God will say to you one day, "Come, O Blessed of my Father, inherit the kingdom prepared for you from the foundation of the world."

I fail to give food to the hungry. I fail to visit the sick. I fail to give water to the thirsty or clothes to the needy, THEN WHAT? Then, says Jesus, God will say to you one day, "Depart from me, you cursed, into the eternal fire prepared for the devil and his angels."

What we do in life—be it as small as a cup of cold water given to an exhausted soul in the name of Christ—has eternal consequences. What we do in this life determines our destiny eternally. It would be good, then, to ask ourselves often: "If I do this, THEN WHAT? What consequences will this act have for me both now and in eternity?"

There would be no sin in the world if people had to taste the bitterness of it first, and the sweetness of it last. Unfortunately, however, the devil places a thin coat of sugar over the bitterness of sin so that we taste its sweetness first and its bitterness last. Someone said once, "Everything has to be paid for in life. Good things are paid for *before* you get them; bad things are paid for *afterwards*." How true this is of life. Love, for example, is paid for in advance in the discipline it costs in being a person capable of loving and worthy of being loved. Lust, on the other hand, is paid for afterwards in remorse, frustration, disappointment, sorrow, and guilt. So before you sin, ask yourself: "What will it cost me in loss of self-respect? How will I feel about it tomorrow? How will I be able to live with myself? How will I feel toward the person with whom or against whom I sinned? How will I feel toward my parents? toward my children? toward my wife? How will I feel toward God? How will He feel toward me?"

A man once boarded a bus to Detroit. After a long trip he got off at his destination only to find himself not in Detroit but in Kansas City. He had caught the wrong bus.

We, too, can catch the wrong bus in life. There is a bus whose destination is: "Let us eat, drink and be merry. . . ." There is another bus which beckons, "Come aboard. Don't be prudish. Everybody's doing it." At first the ride seems good but in the end we realize that this bus has taken us to a place to which we never really wanted to go. "There is a way which seems right to man," says the Bible, "but its end is the way of death."

So before you board any bus in life be like the woman who was going to Chicago. She showed her ticket to the station attendant and asked, "Are you sure this bus will take me to Chicago?" The attendant assured her that it would. When he came by the second and third time she asked him the same question. Irritated, he asked, "I told you once. Why do you keep bothering me?" "Mister," the woman replied, "it'll make a lot of difference tomorrow morning, if I get on the wrong bus tonight."

Let us ask ourselves before we embark on any venture, "If I take this bus, THEN WHAT? Will it take me to the blessed life God wants me to live? Or will it take me somewhere I really don't want to go—to a life of sorrow and regret, to the realization that my life has been worthless?"

Perhaps we should ask this question of each new day: A new day, THEN WHAT? Will it really be a *new* day, or will it be just a continuation of yesterday? Will it find us living in the same old ruts with the same old habits? Or will there be something dynamically *new* about it? There will if we yield our life to Him who can make all things new. "Behold," says Jesus, "I make all things new." "If any man be in Christ he is a *new* creature. . . ." Jesus—the all-powerful, all-sufficient Saviour—can give us a new power, a new peace, a new purpose, a new joy, a new attitude that will make every day *new*.

There are other, more positive ways, to ask ourselves this question: THEN WHAT?

I pray, THEN WHAT? Then, I am talking with God who is not only Creator of this vast universe but who is also my Father and my Friend, who will guide and strengthen me, who loves me and will answer my prayer, perhaps not my way but always in a way that will be best for me. I pray, THEN WHAT? Then God hears! Then God answers!

I read a chapter from the Holy Bible every day, THEN WHAT? Then I am reading God's personal letter to me. I am letting God speak to me. I am allowing Him to give me His guidance, His wisdom, His light for my life.

I participate in the divine liturgy every Sunday, THEN WHAT? Then, I come to Christ. I let Him speak to me through the Gospel and the sermon. I stand in His presence. I ask His forgiveness as did the dying thief. I am present at the Last Supper. I receive from His hand His precious body and blood.

We live and we die, THEN WHAT? Then, says Jesus, comes either heaven or hell. It's as if He were telling us: "Be careful how you live. Ahead of you is heaven but ahead of you is also hell. Life is serious business." One day "we shall all stand before the judgment seat of God ... to give account of ourselves to God" (Rom. 14:10). "Sooner or later," said Robert Louis Stevenson, "everybody sits down to a banquet of consequences."

I choose to live for Christ, THEN WHAT? Then one day I shall come to the end of my life and instead of cursing the darkness I shall be able to say with St. Paul, "The time of my departure has come. I have fought the good fight. I have finished the race. I have kept the faith. Henceforth, there is laid up for me the crown of righteousness, which the Lord, the righteous judge, will award me on that Day, and not only to me but also to all who have loved his appearing."

Chapter Nineteen

THE RICH FOOL

JESUS SPOKE ONCE of an eminently successful man. If he lived in our town today, he would be considered one of the most successful men. And yet the Lord Jesus called this man a fool!

How is it possible for a successful man to be a fool? Success is one of the greatest rewards we strive for in life. And we need rewards. They motivate us. They build up our self-esteem. Success is a normal and necessary part of life. But the question that needs to be answered is: What is real success? When is a person truly successful?

Gerald Kennedy writes, ". . . we assume that any success achieved in any field makes a man an authority in all fields. So the film star is paid for a testimonial about the virtues of a refrigerator. The athlete tells us what kind of hair oil to use. The business tycoon speaks a final word about whiskey. It always seems strange to me that the opinion or taste of any of these people should be taken so seriously in so many places. Surely it is naive to believe that because a man is a first-rate boxer he is to be regarded as an authority on shaving. But success in any field carries great power of persuasion with us in all fields." *

Americans worship success. But I doubt if too many of us know what real success is. For example, the two most notable figures in the history of Africa in the 19th century were Cecil Rhodes and David Livingstone. Rhodes amassed millions exploiting Africa, with its gold and its diamonds. His desire to seize all of South Africa for the British Empire was one of the chief causes of the Boer War. Rhodes died worth many millions of dollars. The other figure was a missionary and ex-

* Kennedy, Gerald, *The Parables* (Harper and Row). By permission.

plorer, Livingstone. He gave his life not only to bring the Gospel of Christ to the black people of Central Africa, but also to fight against slavery and all the oppressions with which they were beset. He died with hardly a penny to his name. Some people consider Rhodes successful; others disagree and consider Livingstone successful.

What do we mean by "success"? Success by whose standards? Jesus tells us that God is the final judge before whom we shall stand one day. He is the One who will proclaim us "successful" or "unsuccessful." And the truly successful according to our Lord are not those who have only a collection of *things* to show for their journey through life but those who are rich in faith and love toward God and man.

Many years ago Rudyard Kipling made a commencement address at McGill University in Montreal. He said one striking thing which deserves to be kept in remembrance. He was warning the students against an overconcern for money, position, or glory. He said: *"Some day you will meet a Man who cares for none of these things. Then you will know how poor you are."*

Jesus once called a "successful" farmer a *fool*. His "success" was nothing more than an accumulation of *"things"* and at last he had nothing but barns to show for it.

This was the first mistake the rich fool made. He mistook bigger barns for success. His second mistake was that he thought he could find an easier life, a more satisfying and peaceful life in bigger barns. "I will pull down my barns and build larger ones ... and I will say to my soul, 'Soul, you have ample goods laid up for many years; take your ease. ...'" But no man finds it easier to live merely because he has enlarged his barns. There is something about big barns that seems to rob life of all peace and serenity. In the midst of all his abundance when the rich farmer should have been at ease, satisfied and content, he was anything but at ease. He was troubled and anxious. "What shall I do with all my crops?" he asked. "Where shall I store them? How shall I protect them?" Fears, worries, anxieties!

He was like a certain Uncle Jim who set out one day to trap some wild turkeys. He rigged up a box as his trap. A

string was tied to a pole that held up the side cover of the
box. Uncle Jim hid in a clump of bushes with the other end
of the string, waiting to spring the trap. There was corn for
bait and soon several turkeys showed up. Eleven of them walked
right into the box, but there was one still outside. So Uncle
Jim waited a while in order to get all twelve, but while he
was waiting, three of the eleven walked out. He wished then
that he had pulled the string when there were eleven. Now
he decided to wait until the three walked back in. But instead
five more walked out. That left only three inside. He was not
satisfied to get three when he might have had eleven, so he
waited patiently for just a few more to go in. Then two more
walked out, and poor Uncle Jim was about ready to have a
nervous breakdown trying to decide whether or not to pull that
string. But before he could make up his mind, the last turkey
walked out and he was left with nothing.

This is why we seldom find *ease* in things. Someone else's
barn will always be bigger than ours; someone else's home will
always look more attractive; someone else's job will always
seem more appealing. We are not content to claim what is
rightly ours; we always want more; so in the end we lose
everything. Happiness is not found in the accumulation of
things. It is not bought and sold in the market place. It is
rather the by-product of a life that is dedicated to Christ. Happiness and peace of soul come when we allow Christ to dwell
in the castle of our soul. Then the barns do not become ends
in themselves. They acquire meaning beyond themselves by
being dedicated to a purpose bigger than themselves—a purpose which helps us realize that the barns and everything in
them are not really ours; they belong to God. He has entrusted
them to our care. He has loaned them to us to use not only
for ourselves but also for our fellow man. One day He will
ask us to render Him an account of how we used them.

The rich fool made three mistakes. First, he mistook bigger
barns for success; second, he thought he could find an easier
and more peaceful life in the fact that he had laid up so many
things for himself; third, he mistook time for eternity. "Soul,
you have ample goods laid up for *many* years." He thought he
had many years. He thought he could hide behind his youth.

He thought the future was his. But the future is never ours. It is God's. ". . . this night your soul is required of you."

It was good that the rich fool spoke to his soul, even though he did not say the right thing, "Soul, you have ample goods laid up for many years. . . ." There are many profitable things that we can say to our soul. We can say, for example, "Soul, you will never succeed in covering your nakedness with an accumulation of things. Only Christ can cover your nakedness with the robe of His grace and forgiveness. Soul, why do you gaze so long and so eagerly at the mud and the dust and the straw and the small stones of this world when over your head Christ holds a golden crown? You will never find ease and peace in building bigger barns. As the Lord of hosts says through the prophet Haggai, '. . . you eat but you never have enough; you drink, but you never have your fill; you clothe yourselves, but no one is warm; and he who earns wages earns wages to put them in a bag with holes' (Hag. 1:6).

"Soul, you will find peace and meaning in life only when you realize that you own nothing; that you are a trustee, a steward of everything: your property, your talents, your over-flowing barns are His. You are to use them so as to be rich toward God, toward your fellow man, and lastly toward your-self." And finally we can say to our soul, "Soul, you were created not only for time but for eternity. Don't lose yourself in this world. Just as you make investments that will pay dividends in time, so commit yourself to Christ. Make invest-ments that will pay dividends throughout eternity. 'What shall it profit a man if he gain the whole world and lose his soul?' For you were created, O Soul, for an eternity where 'eye has not seen, ear has not heard, nor has it ever entered into the heart of man what things God has prepared for those who love him.' "

Chapter Twenty

THE KING IN DISGUISE

IN THE EARLY DAYS there was a king who decided to test the character of his people. Disguised as a peasant, he travelled about his country and was treated for the most part quite shamefully. In time he came to realize that the honor with which his people greeted him as king was not due to the respect they felt for his goodness; rather, it was the result of the fear and awe they felt for his wealth and power.

Finally one day as the king was going about in disguise, one of his subjects recognized him. This subject protested the king's going about like any other man, and insisted that he go back to his throne, put on his royal robes once more, and rule as a proper king should. The people thought it was a sort of trick the king was playing on them to see if he could catch them off guard.

There is another King who travels in disguise—a king who was born in a cave of a poor peasant girl, who lived and worked as a carpenter in the tiny town of Nazareth.

We read in the Gospels that Jesus often "appeared in another form" (Mark 16:12). He appeared to His disciples disguised as an ordinary person. For example, we read of His approaching people in the physical appearance of a person they did not know: to Mary Magdalene He seemed at first sight to be a gardener; it was only after a long conversation with Him that she realized the gardener was Jesus. To the two men walking on the road to Emmaus He appeared as a fellow traveller; it was a long time before they discovered that the person with whom they had been walking was Christ; to the Apostles fishing on the Sea of Galilee He appeared as a stranger. In these ways Jesus was illustrating that He is in all men. He is similar to anyone with whom we might rub elbows today at street-corners, in the supermarket, or on a bus. He is especially in

those who suffer and look to us for assistance. "Truly I say
to you, as you did it to one of these the least of my brethren,
you did it to me."

At the close of World War II, a young American officer
found himself on an island in the South Pacific. On this island
there was a large leper colony. As he wandered around the
separate dwellings he came upon a nun who was dressing the
wounds of one of the lepers. When the soldier saw the infected
legs and running sores he became nauseated. All this was too
much for him, and he exclaimed: "I would not do that for
a million dollars!"

Undisturbed the nun turned towards the young man and replied: "Neither would I!" For a million dollars she would not
touch those running sores, but because Christ dwells in those
outcasts whom society banishes from its sight, she had left home
and wandered thousands of miles to assist those in suffering, to
assist the King in disguise!

There is a legend of St. Francis of Assisi. In his early days
he was very wealthy; nothing but the best was good enough
for him; he was an aristocrat of the aristocrats. But he was ill
at ease and there was no peace in his soul. One day as he was
riding alone outside the city he saw a leper, a mass of sores, a
horrible and a repulsive sight. Ordinarily Francis would have
drawn back in horror from this hideous wreck of humanity.
But something moved within him; he dismounted from his horse
and on an impulse flung his arms around the leper. A moment
later he looked back and there was no one there; only the empty
road in the hot sunlight. All his days thereafter Francis was
sure it was no leper but Christ himself whom he had met and
embraced on that lonely road. It was the King in disguise!

J. D. Salinger in his book *Franny and Zooey* tells of a fat
lady sitting on her porch all day, swatting flies, with her
radio going full blast. He describes her as having "thick legs,
very veiny" and being tormented by cancer. Quite a repulsive
person! Then Salinger asks, ". . . don't you know who that fat
lady really is? . . . It's Christ himself. Christ himself. . . ." The
King in disguise.

Jesus is often pictured as an attractive man—tall, with a
straight nose, friendly eyes, and a radiant face. But the

Gospels suggest that Salinger's picture of Christ as the
fat lady or as the hideous leper may be closer to reality than
the head of Christ as pictured on a beautiful icon. For, you see,
Christ appears to us today in disguise as He did so often in the
Gospels. He comes to us as an ordinary person: as one of the
least of our brethren—the hungry, the naked, the thirsty, the
stranger, the prisoner, the fat lady, the leper. These are the
masks the King wears when He comes in disguise!

"When the Son of Man comes in his glory . . . before him
will be gathered all the nations . . . and he will separate them
one from another . . . to those at his right hand he will say,
'Come, O blessed of my Father, inherit the kingdom prepared
for you from the foundation of the world . . . to those at his left
he will say, 'Depart from me, you cursed, into the eternal
fire prepared for the devil and his angels. . . .' "

The basis on which we shall be judged by God when He
appears at the end of history is: how deeply we loved the King
when He appeared to us in disguise. "Lord, when did we see
thee hungry and feed thee, or thirsty and gave thee drink? Or
when did we see thee a stranger and welcome thee?" And the
King will answer them, "Truly, I say to you, as you did it to
one of the least of these my brethren, you did it to me."

Chapter Twenty-One

THERE ARE NO LITTLE THINGS

LAST YEAR SOMEONE left out a small hyphen and it cost the U.S. government $18,500,000! The hyphen was omitted when feeding instructions to a computer which was to guide a rocket to Venus. The lack of this tiny hyphen sent the rocket off course and it had to be destroyed.

In the movie "The Longest Day," which tells the story of the Allied invasion of France during World War II, a German general asks permission of Hitler to use reserve troops and tanks to counterattack the Allies. He is told, "Hitler has taken a sleeping pill and cannot be disturbed." The angry general mutters, "The fate of Europe is being decided by a sleeping pill."

A tiny hyphen! A sleeping pill! Little things! Yet how important in their consequences. Bruce Barton said once, "Sometimes when I consider what tremendous consequences come from little things . . . I am tempted to think . . . there are no little things."

In the Old Testament book *The Song of Songs* we read of the little foxes which ate the roots of vines and destroyed vineyards. They were rarely seen. It was not the beasts of prey that prowl in the night which brought ruin to the countryside. It was the little foxes.

These same little foxes play a destructive role in the lives of Christians today.

They are active in church. C. S. Lewis in his book *Screwtape Letters* tells of a certain devil who became alarmed when the person he was assigned to guide to hell, suddenly joined a church. He wrote a letter to Satan, his manager, asking him what to do. Satan counseled his agent not to become disturbed but to remain with his man constantly, especially when he was in church. "Keep him aware of *little things*," he said. "Keep him aware of the fact that this usher is a hypocrite, that

this man's shoes squeak, that this lady's hat does not fit properly. Keep him so aware of little things that he will never see
Christ." Little things keep us from Christ.

An Englishman once startled the world by going over Niagara Falls in a barrel without suffering harm. Some years
later this same Englishman was walking down the street,
slipped on an orange peeling, and was taken to the hospital
with a badly fractured leg. A big temptation that roars around
us like Niagara may leave us unharmed. But a little insignificant incident may often cause our downfall simply because
we are not looking for it.

When Jesus speaks of the Last Judgment, He does not
mention at all the great sins—adultery, murder, stealing. He
speaks rather of the little sins of omission. "I was a stranger
and you did not wlecome me, naked and you did not clothe
me, sick and in prison and you did not visit me." "I didn't
kill anyone," we often say. Perhaps not. But if we consider
the little sins of omission, the good we could have done but did
not, who of us is guiltless? The little foxes are the ones that
destroy the vine.

A bishop said once, "The trouble with some of us Christians
is that we have great convictions about little things." A survey
was made at a certain college to discover what the greatest
concern of the college students was. It was found that the greatest concern of these' particular college students was finding a
place to park the car! Great convictions about little things . . .
to the point where the whole purpose of life is so easily missed.

If you have read *Gulliver's Travels* you will remember that
Gulliver was a giant who lived among the pigmies. But the
little pigmies managed to tie him down flat on the earth by a
thousand little strings. Gulliver reflects most of us. We are
created by God to be giants but we allow ourselves to be tied
down by a thousand little strings to a thousand little things.

As Fred W. Newman wrote,

> "I've got my ulcers
> And numerous ills
> From mountain climbing
> On molehills."

It's the little foxes that cause the greatest destruction.

What makes a happy home? Mostly little things. When your children come home from school and want to tell you something, stop everything you're doing and listen to them—even if it means a burned cake in the oven. For if you don't listen to the little things your children wish to tell you now, they'll never come to you later with the big problems. What children need most is not bigger toys but little things like time: time for listening, time for understanding, time for helping, time for guiding.

What causes many marriages to fail? Mostly little things. Little discourtesies, little acts of selfishness and indifference and grudgefulness that wear on a marriage so that love is at last destroyed.

What causes so many marriages to succeed? Mostly little things. The little acts of kindness and thoughtfulness that we do for each other, the small remembrances and gifts of affection, the words of appreciation and praise for each other—these provide the happy memories which every marriage needs if it is to prosper. If it is the little things that tear a marriage apart bit by bit, it is also little things that build it up and strengthen it.

Many times some of us feel that we have to do big things for Jesus in order to please Him. We forget that it was Jesus who said that "even a cup of cold water given in my name will have its reward." Even little acts of love such as a visit to the sick, He considers so important as to say, "You did it to me."

A doctor once pointed to a rather worn teddy bear in his office and said, "That is the highest fee I ever received for a case. Years ago a poor mother brought me her little girl who had gone blind. She could not afford the expensive operation, but I took the case anyway. Every time they visited the office, the little girl was carrying the teddy bear. Nothing in the world seemed to mean so much to her. On the day when her eyes were finally uncovered and she was able to see again, she looked at her precious teddy bear, and then, coming over to me she placed it in my hand as a token of her gratitude. I have never received a larger fee than that for any case." Little things

—yet how expressive they can be of love, devotion and gratitude!

What is "the best portion of a good man's life?"

Wordsworth answers:

"His little nameless, unremembered acts

Of kindness and of love."

God cares for little things. He cares for tiny sparrows: "Not one sparrow falls to the ground unless it be the Father's will." He cared for the poor widow who placed just two pennies in the Temple offering box. He praised her because those two pennies represented all her substance. He cares for little people—the blind, the lepers, the lame, the forgotten ones. For Him there are no little people. They are all His children. For them He died on the cross. For them He has prepared the kingdom in heaven.

One day a friend asked Michelangelo what work he had done on a certain statue since he had seen it last. "I have touched this, polished that, softened this feature, brought out that muscle," answered Michelangelo.

"But these are such little things," said the friend.

"Yes, they are," answered Michelangelo, "but it is little things that make perfection, and perfection is not a little thing."

"Sometimes when I consider what tremendous consequences come from little things . . . I am tempted to think . . . there are no little things."—Bruce Barton.

Chapter Twenty-Two

THREE PICTURES

I WISH TO HOLD UP BEFORE YOU three pictures. The first picture is painted by Dr. Viktor Frankl, famous Viennese psychiatrist, in his now classic book, *Man's Search for Meaning*. He tells of his experiences as a Jew in a Nazi concentration camp. The prisoners had been packed like cattle into a box car and shipped to concentration camps. When they arrived at the camp, naked, starving, reeking with filth, each one had to file past a senior S. S. officer. The officer had assumed an attitude of careless ease, supporting his right elbow with his left hand. His right hand was lifted and as each prisoner walked by him he would point very leisurely either to the right or to the left. If he pointed to the right side, the person would be sent to a work camp. If the finger pointed to the left side, it meant that each person was given a bar of soap and asked to enter a building which had the word "bath" written over its doors. The "bath" turned out to be a gas chamber where these people were gassed and later burned in ovens. One prisoner did not know what happened to a friend. A colleague asked him, "Was he sent to the left side?"

"Yes," replied the man.

"Then you can see him there," he was told.

"Where?"

A hand pointed to the chimney a few hundred yards off, which was sending a sinister cloud of smoke into the grey sky of Poland. "That's where your friend is, floating up to heaven," was the answer.

The second picture is taken from a recent issue of one of our national magazines. It shows a man standing alone on an ice floe surrounded by a vast emptiness. He looks utterly abandoned. The picture is used to express what a certain group of people who call themselves Existentialists (not the Christian

Existentialists) believe about man. They believe that man is utterly alone in the universe. There is no God who cares; no one to help him. There is no destiny but only that which man makes for himself.

The third picture is found in the Gospels. It concerns a woman who had a hemorrhage for twelve years. Any such woman in Jewish society was unclean. Everything and everyone she touched became infected with that uncleanness. She was absolutely shut off from the worship of God and from the fellowship of other men and women. This woman should not have been in that crowd surrounding Jesus, for she was infecting with her uncleanness everyone whom she touched. There is little wonder, then, that she was desperately eager to try anything which would rescue her from this life of isolation and humiliation.

She said to herself as she saw Jesus, "If I only touch his garment I will be cured." She approached Jesus. When she touched His garment, she felt a surge of healing power in her body. Suddenly, Jesus stopped. For a moment it seemed that for Him no one but that woman and nothing but her need existed. She was not simply a poor woman who was lost in that crowd; she was someone to whom Jesus gave the whole of himself. For Jesus who is God no one is ever lost in a crowd; no one is ever lost in the vastness of the universe. The love of God is infinite for every human soul. Each person is God's individual child. God has invested His image in each one of us. Each one of us has all of God's love, all of God's care and power at his disposal. Jesus turned to this woman and said, "Daughter, thy faith has saved thee; go in peace."

Three pictures!

Picture No. 1. People being sent to gas chambers by the mere pointing of a finger.

Picture No. 2. A man standing on an ice floe utterly alone in a sea of nothingness.

Picture No. 3. The Lord Jesus stopping and responding to the need of a woman who was seemingly lost in a crowd.

"What is man that thou art mindful of him," asks the writer of Hebrews. "And the son of man that thou carest for him? For thou has made him a little lower than the angels and hast crowned him with glory and honor."

Man is not an animal to be dispensed with by the pointing of a finger. Man is not alone in this universe overpowered by the absurdity of death. Man, every man, is the perpetual concern of God who sacrificed His beloved Son for him on Calvary, that "whosoever believes in him should not perish but have everlasting life." And every man should be our perpetual concern. For in every man there is the image of God. Every man is the man for whom Christ died.

Chapter Twenty-Three

NO PLOT, BUT WHAT A CAST!

A PERSON LOOKED OVER the New York City telephone book one day and said, "No plot, but what a cast!"

The Lord Jesus has a great plot for mankind: "that all should be saved and come to the knowledge of truth." The Gospels tell how Jesus began enlisting a cast to carry out His plot. He came upon some common, ordinary, ignorant, smelly fishermen mending their nets and He said to them, "Follow me and I will make you fishers of men." "Immediately they left their nets and followed him." To that original cast of twelve we owe the spread of Christianity today.

We have at least one thing in common with those first twelve disciples. Jesus directs to us today the same invitation He extended those twelve fishermen: "Follow Me." He has a plot—the greatest plot in the world. He needs a cast. He calls us to be that cast.

What does it mean to follow Christ today? It means, of course, to abide with Him in the church, in the Sacraments, in prayer, in Bible study. But it means more than this. It means that the time we spend with Jesus in church and in prayer affects everything we do during the week. It means that we take Christ with us to our homes, to our work, into our marriage, into our everyday relationships with our children, our employer, our employees.

Perhaps a few examples will help us understand how this can be done. A Christian layman was waiting in line to register at one of New York City's great hotels. Immediately in front of him was a nicely dressed and, as it turned out, a cultured-speaking Negro. When the Negro reached the desk, he asked the clerk for a room. "No," was the reply, "all the rooms are filled." Without a word the colored gentleman turned away. Up stepped the man behind him. He purposely used the same words the colored man used: "I should like to have a room." "Yes," said the clerk, "what price would you like?" At that, the Christian layman called to the colored man, who was making his way across the lobby. "Please come back," he called, "this man made a mistake. The rooms aren't all sold because he just gave me one." Then he turned to the clerk and said quietly but firmly, "Do you want me to sue you or not? I'm ready to sue you right now." The clerk answered hastily, "Very well, he can have a room."

"Follow Me." This modern disciple followed Christ by practicing in a hotel lobby the Christian faith he confessed in church on Sunday morning.

I wonder how many of us would have had the courage to do that. Most of us would have let the incident pass, saying, "Oh well, that's none of my business." Six million Jews were slaughtered in Germany because Christians sat back and said, "Oh well, what can I do? It's none of my business!" We got rid of Hitler but we did not get rid of Hitlerism—his pride, his arrogance, his vindictiveness, his racial hatred, his defiance of God's Word. And some Hitler will come again unless Christians really begin to follow Christ, taking Him into their business, into their politics, into their race relations, into their lives.

Another example. Here was a young woman, crippled by polio, unable to walk. Her only means of communication was by mail and telephone. Knowing depressing loneliness first-hand, she decided to do something for others who felt the same way. She contacted the state rehabilitation agent who gave her the names and addresses of other shut-ins. She began calling them regularly. From the local hospital, she obtained the names of people awaiting surgery and, by phone or mail, she contacted them to tell them, "Someone cares and is praying for you." She made the love of Christ real to them.

"Follow Me." This modern disciple who knew firsthand the pain of loneliness followed Christ, devoting her life to spreading the love of Christ and His care to other shut-ins.

A final example. One of the great stories of the Christian Church is the story of Telemachus, a Christian monk. One day he went to Rome. He found his way to the gladiatorial games where men fought with each other till death. The crowds roared with the lust for blood, much as they do in boxing today. Eighty thousand people were there to view the gladiator's fight to the finish. Telemachus was horrified. Were not these men who were slaughtering each other children of God? And were not those who were cheering them on, lusting for blood, encouraging murder? He leapt from his seat right into the arena, and stood between the gladiators. "This is wrong," he called out, "it is against God's law." He was tossed aside. He came back. The crowd was angry. They began to stone him. Soon he lay dead in the arena. Then suddenly there was a hush. The crowd realized what had happened. A holy man lay dead. Something happened that day to Rome, for there were never any gladiatorial games any more. All because an unknown monk, Telemachus, stood up to protest to the world something he knew was against God's will.

"Follow me," said Christ. Telemachus followed Him even at the cost of his life.

Who will follow Christ today to make real His love to a love-starved world, to bring the message of His forgiveness to a world perishing with guilt. Who will follow Him to make right the wrongs in today's society, to protest the evil, to affirm the truth, to protect the afflicted?

"God so loved the world that he gave his only begotten Son that whoever believes in him may not perish but have life everlasting." What a plot! But where is the cast? "Follow me," says Christ. You are the cast.

"Whom shall I send?" said the Lord to Isaiah. Isaiah replied, "Here am I, Lord. Send me!"

Chapter Twenty-Four

GOD IS NOT DEAD!

A LITTLE GIRL HAD BEEN ATTENDING Sunday school where she made a little plaque with the words, "Have Faith in God" as a motto. She boarded the bus that would take her to her home, and as the bus was starting to move, she realized that she did not have her little motto with her. She jumped from her seat and dashing up the aisle to the driver shouted, "Stop the bus, I've lost my 'Faith in God.'"

We are living in a day when many people have lost their faith in God. Because they have lost their faith, some of them are proclaiming that God is dead. Newspapers have been carrying a series of articles on the views of certain pseudo-Christian theologians who are proclaiming that God is dead. They do not mean that God is unreal to people, or that the word "God" has lost its meaning; they mean that God is actually dead.

Now this is nothing really new. People who have lost their faith in God have always proclaimed that He was dead. It was Nietzsche who orignated the expression, "God is dead." Someone quipped about him,

"God is dead."

signed, Nietzsche

"Nietzsche is dead."

signed, God

"God is dead!" said Nietzsche. Karl Marx agreed. And communism was born.

"God is dead," said Nietzsche. Camus, Sartre and other atheistic existentialists agreed. And the philosophy of the meaninglessness of life was born. Life is described in terms of "dread," "absurd," "nausea." Camus says that man is like Sisyphus, the Greek mythological character, who was doomed to roll a rock forever up a hill; just when it got to the top, it rolled down and he had to start all over again. The only solution, according to Camus, is for man to fall in love with this rock. This is what life without God is to atheistic existentialists.

"God is dead," said Nietzsche. Freud agreed. And another god came into being: the god of sex, before whose altar millions prostrate themselves—not a normal, wholesome, sacred sex, but an abnormal, disgusting, neurotic, nauseating and sick sex.

"God is dead," said Nietzsche. "If God is dead," said Dostoievski, "then man is god." Man agreed: "I am my own god," he said. And he proceeded to set up his own commandments. There is no right or wrong but what man decides is right or wrong in each situation. The ten commandments are laughed at. There is a breakdown of law and order. There is disrespect for authority—the authority of the state, the police, the university. For, you see, if God is dead, there is not much authority left anywhere.

"God is dead," said Nietzsche. And even Christians believed him. A German pastor writes, "In Germany today there are thousands of *church-member atheists* who have no incentive to participate in any service, who no longer pray." Is it not true today that for many who "belong" to Christian churches God is dead? The question of whether God exists simply does not matter to them. They live their lives without any serious reference to God. Before we criticize these people, however, let us look to ourselves and ask ourselves: When I go back to work, or to school tomorrow, will my belief in God make any difference in the way I act?

If some people today believe that God is dead, could it be that we Christians are to blame? Could it be that we are the ones who have buried Christ in our churches, our creed, our liturgy, our icons and our Bibles? We have hidden the light of Christ under a bushel and have made the world believe that darkness is the only reality.

There is an old Danish fable which tells how a spider slid down a single filament of web from the timbers of a barn and established himself on a lower level. There he spread his web, caught flies, grew sleek and prospered. One day he saw the single thread that stretched up into the darkness above him. He thought, "How useless! What purpose does this serve!" and he snipped it. But his web collapsed and soon both the spider and the web were trodden under foot.

This is what happens to man when he severs the tie that binds him to God. When God dies, man dies; man's freedom dies; man's dignity dies; man's worth as an individual dies, as it has died today wherever atheistic communism rules.

But God is not dead! One of the greatest space experts alive today, Dr. Werner Von Braun, acknowledges that he is a believer in the Lord Jesus. When asked how he came to the full conviction of the fact of God, he said, "I came to it through science; I could not deny the evidence." Dr. Von Braun sees the evidence of God in science. Others do not. Having eyes, they see not.

Frederick Buechner says that if God suddenly rearranged the stars of the Milky Way to spell out in huge letters the words: I REALLY EXIST, or GOD IS, many people would probably fall on their knees and believe. But after a while they would become so accustomed to those words in the sky that they would say, "So what if God exists! What difference does that make?"

The greatest evidence of God for Orthodox Christians is not science or the Milky Way but the Christ who lives, reigns, rules and conquers. He is the LIVING LORD, THE PANTO-CRATOR.

GOD IS NOT DEAD! Speaking to Moses in the Old Testament He said, "I *have seen* the affliction . . . I have *heard* the cry of the people . . . I *know* their sorrows . . ." (Ex. 3:7, 8). God is aware, so aware, so concerned that He said, "*I am come down* to deliver them. . . ." Again and again God came down to meet man in his need. His greatest coming down was in the historic life, death and resurrection of Christ. "That which we have *heard*, which we have *seen* with our eyes, which we have *looked* upon and *touched* with our hands . . . we proclaim also to you," writes the Apostle John (I John 1:1–3).

One day the Apostle Philip said to Jesus, "Show us the Father and we will be satisfied; then we will believe." Jesus chided Philip, saying in effect, "God the Father is not going to come down at every request that man makes to see Him. God has been revealed in history, Philip, and now in Me. He who sees Me, sees the Father."

GOD IS NOT DEAD! We believe in a risen Lord, a living Lord, an all-powerful Lord! "God also hath highly exalted him, and given him a name which is above every name, that at the name of Jesus every knee should bow, of things in heaven, and things in earth, and things under the earth, and that every tongue should confess that Jesus Christ is Lord, to the glory of God the Father" (Phil. 2:9–11).

GOD IS NOT DEAD! It is no weak Christ with whom we have to do, but a Christ of power! When Stephen was being stoned to death, he looked up to heaven and saw "the son of man standing at the right hand of God." He saw the living, triumphant Christ! It was this vision that made him a hero. With his bodily eyes he saw men stoning him, but with the eyes of the spirit he saw Jesus, enthroned and ruling over the world; even over the present horror in which he, Stephen, was dying.

It is this vision of our risen Lord and King of all creation which gives to every faithful Christian a courage, a confidence, a hope, and a faith which no other man can have. The vision of a living, reigning Lord! With that vision we can endure anything, for we know that the present pain or terror cannot be final. Our Lord will give us the eternal victory.

In these perilous times, where can we go? Where can we go for peace in a world where there is no peace? Where can we go for permanence in a world where we live from moment to moment? Where can we go for shelter in a world where there is no place to hide? Where else but to Him who is "our rock and our salvation, our fortress. . . ." "Trust in him at all times," says the psalmist. "Pour out your heart before him. God is our refuge and strength."

GOD IS NOT DEAD! But He can be dead for you if you want Him to be. Then you, too, will die. Your freedom will die. Your dignity will die. Your self-respect will die. Your hope will die. Your courage will die. Your strength will die. You will die.

The problem of our age is not the "death of God" but rather the death of man. And man is dying because he has tried too long to live without God.

Dag Hammarskjold writes in his book, *Markings*, "God does not die on the day we cease to believe in a personal deity, *but we die* on the day when our lives cease to be illumined by the steady radiance, renewed daily, of a wonder, the source of which is beyond all reason." *

One day when many disciples left Jesus and would no longer walk with Him, Jesus turned to the twelve and said, "Will you also go away?" To which Simon Peter answered, "Lord, to whom shall we go? You alone have the words of eternal life" (John 6:67).

To those who are proclaiming the death of God, we need to repeat the words the angel addressed to the women who were on their way to the tomb of Jesus: "Why do you seek the living among the dead?"

---

* Hammarskjold, Dag, *Markings;* translated by Leif Sjoberg and W. H. Auden (© Copyright 1964 by Alfred Knopf, Inc., and Faber and Faber Ltd.). Reprinted by permission of the publisher.

Chapter Twenty-Five

EVERY MAN A KING!

SOME TIME AGO newspapers carried the following news item.

A police officer, seeing a fast-moving car, gave chase. When he drew alongside, he shouted to the lady behind the wheel to "pull over to the curb."

"I can't stop the car," she cried out.

"Turn off the ignition key," he directed.

"I can't find it," she shouted back.

Within seconds the car careened down a hill. The bewildered driver couldn't cope with the curve at the bottom. She crashed into a pole and was killed.

It is a fearful thing when a human being loses mastery of anything over which he or she should have control.

Whether it's a speeding car or the deadly passions of pride, greed or lust, man flirts with catastrophe if he allows himself to be dominated by those things over which God created him to be master.

It was said that Frederick the Great of Prussia was walking along a road on the outskirts of Berlin one day when he accidentally brushed against a very old man.

"Who are you?" the king asked out of idle curiosity as the walk came to an abrupt halt.

"I am a king," the old man answered.

"A king? Over what principality do you reign?" asked the amazed Frederick.

"Over myself," replied the elderly man. "I rule myself because I control myself. I am my own subject to command."

Every person is created to be a king. When God made man and woman He said to them: "Replenish the earth and subdue it; and have dominion over the fish of the sea, and over the fowl of the air, and over every living thing that moveth upon the earth" (Gen. 1:28). Through science man today has indeed become master and king of the earth. Now he is even venturing into space. But the tragedy is that, in spite of all this, man is unable to control himself. We are like Alexander the Great who at age 23 had conquered the world. He even wept because there were no more worlds to conquer. He was king of everything and everyone. There was only one thing he was not able to master—himself. In the end Alexander the Great who conquered the world was conquered by alcohol.

Today we who have conquered the world through science are in danger of being conquered by self. We have controlled nature, but are we able to control such a little thing as the tongue? We control water by building huge dams, but are we able to control alcohol or sex? We have controlled atomic power, but are we able to control our teen-agers, our family life, our appetites? Is man the king God created him to be?

"I have had more trouble with myself than with anyone else I ever knew." The person who said these words spoke for all of us. Most often when we get into trouble, we have no one to blame but ourselves. For all the dangers and temptations of the world have no power over us until we let them come into our soul and enslave us.

One of the greatest things in the world is to be master of yourself, so that you do not let anybody else push you around, so that you do not let any of your desires or weaknesses overpower you. There is nothing greater than to be what God created you to be: *king of yourself!*

One of the greatest kings and rulers the world has ever seen wrote, "He that ruleth his own spirit is greater than he that taketh a city." The greatest city of all is to be found beneath every human breast. He who takes that city, and rules it, is the king of all conquerors.

There was an old man who often complained of pain and weariness at the end of the day. A friend asked him why he complained so, and the old man replied, "I have so much to do every day. I have two falcons to tame, two rabbits to keep from running away, two hawks to manage, a serpent to confine, a lion to chain, and a sick man to tend and wait upon."

"Why, you must be joking," said his friend. "Surely no man can have all these things to do at once."

"Indeed I am not joking," said the old man, "but what I

have told you is the sad, sober truth; for the two falcons are
my two eyes, which I must diligently guard; the two rabbits
are my feet, which I must keep from walking in the ways of
sin; the two hawks are my two hands, which I must train to
work, that I may be able to provide for myself and for my
brethren in need; the serpent is my tongue, which I always
bridle lest it speak unseemly; the lion is my heart, with which
I have a continued fight, lest evil things come out of it; and the
sick man is my whole body, which is always needing my watch-
fulness and care. All this daily work wears out my strength."

It is no easy thing to be king of oneself. It requires discipline, restraint, self-denial. It requires that we say "no" to
our bodily instincts and appetites. Outstanding teachers of every age have advised men to take upon themselves every day
some little thing that is disagreeable or unpleasant, so that
they may always retain mastery over their impulses. And this
is what the Orthodox Church encourages us to do with its
emphasis on fasting. No man can become king of himself without self-denial.

Sir Edwin Arnold, author of *The Light of Asia*, speaking
once to the students of Harvard College, said: "In 1776 you
conquered your fathers (referring to the war of the Revolution). In 1861 you conquered your brothers. Now the next
great victory is to conquer yourselves." Is not this always our
greatest victory?

The great Scotch educator Henry Drummond was once
speaking to a driver of horses who was anything but king of
himself; he was an alcoholic, a helpless slave to the bottle.
"What if I who ride beside you," said Drummond, "were the
finest horseman that ever drove a team of horses; what if I
could control the wildest horses that ever pulled a carriage;
what if these horses driven by you were such that you could
not control them; you were helpless, and I said, 'Give me the
reins and I'll control them,' what would you do?"

The man saw the point and said, "Is that what Jesus will
do for a defeated, helpless man like me?"

"That's right," said Drummond. "Let Christ have the reins,
turn your life over to Him and He will make you a king—
the kind of king He created you to be!"

Chapter Twenty-Six

"I BELIEVE,
HELP THOU MY UNBELIEF"

A FATHER BROUGHT HIS SICK SON to Jesus with the faint hope that Jesus would cure him. The boy, said the father, was possessed of a dumb spirit, "and whenever it seizes him it throws him down, he foams at the mouth, grinds his teeth and turns rigid" (Mark 9:18).

Jesus said, "Bring him to me." One of the secrets of life is found in this little phrase, "Bring him to me." When we have a sickness or a problem we always have someone to whom we can go. "Come unto me all ye who labor and are heavy laden and I will give you rest."

As the boy stood before Jesus, he suddenly had an attack. The father looked into the gentle face of the Galilean, and said, *"If you can do anything, have pity on us and help us."* The important words here are *"if you can."* The father doubted that Jesus could actually heal his son. His disciples had tried to heal him just a short time before, and had failed.

There are many today who are like this father! The cynics, for example, whose motto is: "It can't be done." Before the era of open-heart surgery, there were those who said, "It can't be done!" Before the airplane, there were those who said of the Wright brothers and their flying machine, "It can't be done!"

Always, somewhere, somebody has said it: "It'll never work." But look about you. Look at the radio, look at television, look at the medical techniques, look at the countless home and industrial devices. Somewhere someone has said, "It will never work." But it has worked and it does work. Finite man has made it work. If finite man can work these miracles, then who are we to shut the door on Almighty God and say that anything is impossible with Him, that there is no healing power in faith?

"If you can do anything, have pity on us and help us," said the father. But Jesus immediately challenged the father:

"If you can believe! All things are possible to him who believes." The question is not whether or not I have the power to heal your sickness; the question is whether or not you can believe. "All things are possible to him who believes."

A locomotive has tremendous power. It is capable of pulling a long chain of cars to their destination. But the train of cars will not move as long as the coupling that connects the cars with the locomotive is separated. Without that coupling or link, the chain of cars would stand and rust on those rails. So it is with our faith in Christ; it is the coupling that links us to His power.

When Jesus challenged the father saying, *"If you can believe! All things are possible to him who believes,"* at that moment faith was born in the father. With tears streaming down his cheeks he cried, *"Lord, I believe; help my unbelief."* Faith became the coupling linking the father to God's almighty power. His son was healed. Where doubt says: "It can't be done," faith says, "All things are possible to him who believes."

Notice one important fact! When the father said, *"Lord, I believe; help my unbelief,"* he showed that there was still unbelief in his belief. He had not gone from utter unbelief to perfect belief. In this earthly life, there is no such thing as perfect belief. The greatest saints speak of the "dark night of the soul." They speak of a great soul struggle between faith and doubt. To say then that we have doubts is simply another way of saying that we are human. A Christian has no more reason to be ashamed of such doubts than he has reason to be ashamed of his faith. The two are inseparable. But here we must distinguish between two kinds of doubt. There is the doubt of the believer and there is the doubt of the unbeliever. The doubt of the believer is a healthy doubt. It acknowledges that we do not know everything about our faith. It leads us on to more knowledge and, therefore, to growth.

Our young people in college experience this kind of doubt about their faith. It is a normal part of growing up. Their faith is passing through the normal crisis of growth. Such doubt, we hope, will lead our college young people to re-examine their faith intelligently.

A Sunday school teacher once asked her class, "Why do you believe in God?" One child answered, "I guess it just runs in our family."

Faith should never be something that "runs in the family," something we inherit from our parents. Faith is something each person must accept for himself. It is not something that is given to us at baptism. Faith means decision—a personal decision: am I going to rely ultimately on myself or am I going to rely on God? Am I going to trust God's Word or not, believe in Him or not believe? Faith is always a decision—not my parents' decision or anyone else's decision, but my own personal decision to trust God.

While we are speaking of college students, I would like to address myself briefly to those who say that science and faith are irreconcilable. It is not only religion that is based on faith; science is also based on faith. The scientist who is engaged in cancer research bases his whole research on faith—the faith that a cure for cancer exists. He doesn't know that there is such a cure; he believes that such a cure exists. Dr. Jonas E. Salk believed God had placed in this intelligent universe a vaccine to help cure the dreadful disease of polio. He began with faith. His whole research was based on faith. Almost every scientist begins with faith. He begins with a theory, a guess, a hypothesis, and he goes on from there to seek a conclusion. A scientist believes first in order that he may know later.

When someone says, "Prove God to me and I will believe," we ask, "What do you mean by proof? Do you mean logical proof? Is God a geometric theorem to be proved logically? Do you mean scientific proof? Is God a material substance we can place in a test tube and analyze? There are different kinds of proofs for different things. As George Buttrick said, "There is one kind of proof for potatoes, another for poems, another for persons, another for God." The proof for God is to discover Him for yourself, not through logic or science but by faith, by surrendering your life to Him, by prayer, through the Bible, the Church and the Sacraments. These are the tools we use to discover God who is Spirit and Truth. We use spiritual tools to discover spiritual truths. Faith in God is never irrational, never against reason; it is beyond reason;

therefore, beyond logic and beyond scientific demonstration. After all, if we could analyze God in a test tube and understand Him logically, He wouldn't be God. We would be God. He would be less than we are. We would be greater.

So faith is a decision, a decision to trust God and link up my life to His healing, strengthening power. Unbelief, on the other hand, is also a decision, a decision not to trust God; to trust in myself, in Karl Marx, in Freud, in anyone else but God. Faith is a great leap, but unbelief is also a great leap. The difference is that one leads into the darkness of anxiety, the other into the light and certainty of God.

Each morning when we awaken we can face the day either with unbelief or with faith. We can face the day by saying, "I can't make it today. There are problems to face that I just can't overcome. There are temptations that will bowl me over." Anyone who thinks such thoughts can never win. He is defeated before he begins.
• But there is another alternative we can choose. We can begin our day with faith, by getting in tune with God and saying, "Lord, I commit my life to you this day. I believe you are going to be with me every step I take; I believe that you will give me the power I need to be victorious."

In the words of the poet:

> Canst thou take the barren soil
> And with all thy pains and toil
>   make lilies grow?
> Thou canst not, O helpless man,
> Have faith in God. He can!
>
> Canst thou paint the clouds at eve,
> And all the sunset colors weave into
>   the sky?
> Thou canst not, O powerless man.
> Have faith in God. He can!
>
> Canst thou still thy troubled heart
> And make all cares and doubts depart
>   from out thy soul?
> Thou canst not, O faithless man,
> Have faith in God. He can!

When an airliner comes to an airport that is enveloped by fog, it makes an instrument landing. The pilot flies through the thick fog, unable to see a thing. He relies on the signals that are sent out from the airport to guide him. He is not flying blind; he is flying by faith. He believes in those signals and follows them until they lead him to a safe landing at his destination.

We have been placed in this world by God. He loves us. He cares for us. He has given us the greatest proof of His love: the Cross. In moments when clouds gather in our lives and storms develop and trouble looms, we are not called upon to fly blind; we, too, fly by faith, faith that God loves us and wants to help us reach our destination; faith that God's love sends signals to guide us through the fog of life. We shall trust these signals—these promises God has given us—and we shall follow them to a safe landing one day in His eternal kingdom.

Chapter Twenty-Seven

PASCHA! THE GREAT PASSOVER!

WHAT IS EASTER?

Is it a day when everybody dresses up? Is it a holiday? Is it the coming of spring and the end of winter? Is it flowers?

It is all these things. But these are only signs of the main thing. Easter is *life—new life* in Christ Jesus. Easter speaks and demonstrates the great word of Christianity, perhaps the greatest—*life*. "In him [Christ] was *life;* and the *life* was the *light* of men."

At the midnight Easter liturgy the darkness of the sanctuary is annihilated by the light of hundreds of candles. All this light emanates from the altar, from the Paschal Candle representing Christ. Thus the very candles worshippers bear at Easter represent Christ, "the *life* that was the *light* of men."

The Jewish and Greek word for Easter, *Pascha*, means passover, a passage. It refers to the passage of the Jews from the slavery of Egypt to freedom, from exile into the Promised Land. For us Christians the word Pascha means the ultimate passage from sin to salvation, from death to life through the resurrection of our Lord Jesus Christ.

PASCHA! We have passed from death to life. The tomb which could not hold the Lord cannot hold those who live and believe in Him. We place our loved ones in coffins knowing that we shall see them again. We bury them in the earth confident that it will not consume them eternally, confident of that day of resurrection when the dead in Christ shall rise to live eternally in bodies that have been redeemed from corruption.

PASCHA! The Great Passover! We have passed from death to life!

Yet the resurrection is not something that will take place in the future. Eternal life is not something that begins after we die. It begins now and continues on into eternity. It begins now when we take Christ into our life as Saviour and Lord. It begins now when we establish a living, personal relationship with Christ, speaking to Him every day in prayer; reading His personal letter to us—the Holy Bible; meeting Him personally in each one of the Sacraments; abiding with Him every Sunday in the Eucharist; ministering to Him personally in the least of His brethren. As Jesus said, "Inasmuch as you have done it to one of the least of these my brethren, you have done it to me."

For some the thought that life will go on forever is too dreadful to contemplate. Life is so distasteful to them that *they cannot bear to think* that it will go on forever. These are people who go through the motions of living but who might as well be dead and buried. They are dead in their spirits, dead in their minds, dead in their hope. What they need is a resurrection, a personal resurrection! What they need is to take Christ, the *life*, into their lives and let Him resurrect them to a new life. The resurrection is not merely a commemoration, solemn and beautiful, of a past event. It is a contemporary experience being demonstrated constantly in those who take Jesus into their lives as Lord and Saviour. He resurrects us now. He gives us a new quality of life, a new power over sin, a new perspective, a new joy, a new peace, a new love. Witness Paul resurrected from persecutor to Apostle. Witness Zacchaeus resurrected from selfish, greedy, conniving thief to philanthropist. Witness Mary Magdalene resurrected from woman of the streets to saint. Take Christ and *live*. "In him was *life*; and the *life* was the *light* of men."

Of course, it all depends on what we mean by *life*. For some it means ambition and power. For others it means going out and having themselves a time. I think it was Dante who wrote in the "Inferno" about a young couple who wanted nothing in life but each other in immoral, illicit love. In hell, for eternity, that was exactly what they had—each other, days without end, unadorned, naked and alone. That for them was not life but hell. So let us be careful what we desire—what we place first in life; God may give it to us exclusively for all eternity. For He is a great respecter of human freedom.

   PASCHA, the great Passover. We have passed from death to
life, from sin to salvation, from weakness to power.

   The *Pascha* (passover) of the Lord,
   From death unto life,
   And from earth unto heaven
   Has Christ our God brought us over. . . .

   Now are all things filled with light,
   Heaven and earth and the places under the earth.
   All Creation does celebrate the Resurrection of Christ.
   On whom it is founded. . . .

   We celebrate the death of Death,
   The annihilation of Hell,
   The beginning of a new life and everlasting.
   And with ecstasy we sing praises to the author thereof. . . .

   This is the chosen and holy Day,
   The one King and Lord of Sabbaths,
   The Feast of Feasts and the Triumph of Triumphs. . . .

   O Christ, the Passover great and most holy!
   O Wisdom, Word and Power of God!
   Grant that we may more perfectly partake of Thee
   In the day of Thy Kingdom which knoweth no night.

                              —From the *Orthodox Easter Matins*

Chapter Twenty-Eight

FAILURE:
TEACHER OR UNDERTAKER?

A YOUNG MAN SAT in the pastor's office completely dejected. "Why did I do it?" he kept asking. "How could I make such a terrible mistake? What in the world is wrong with me? Haven't I any sense at all? Here I had the opportunity of a lifetime and I blew it! I have ruined my future."

Jesus tells of another young man who failed—the Prodigal Son. He took his inheritance, wasted it in riotous living and ended up feeding swine. Who is it who does not fail at times? In fact, failure seems to be more a part of life for most of us than success is. How does a Christian deal with failure?

The first thing we need to remember is that it is human to fail. Only God does not make mistakes. Someone once said, "Your failure may make you feel like the devil, but this is because you spend too much of your time feeling like God." In the early Church there was a group of people called the Donatists. They believed that the Christian Church should be composed only of perfect Christians who did not sin. So they expelled from the Church those who had sinned. Thus, the Church for the Donatists became a club where only the righteous could belong. But the Church condemned the Donatists. The true Church of Christ is not a club for the righteous but a hospital where those who are sick come to the Great Physician for healing. So the Church is composed not of perfect Christians but of those who have failed and know they have failed.

A monk was asked once, "What do you do there in the monastery?" He replied, "We fall and get up, fall and get up, fall and get up again." A Christian is not one who does not fall; he is one who rises after each fall.

When Mr. McNamara became Secretary of Defense, Henry Ford II commented that the Ford Company was successful because it was approximately fifty-one percent right in its judgments and decisions. This means that it was wrong a staggering forty-nine percent of the time!

All of us remember Babe Ruth because he hit more than 700 home runs in his major league career. But we forget that he struck out—he failed—more than 3,000 times.

All of us—from the littlest monk, to great ball players, to the greatest corporations—make mistakes. All of us err. All of us sin. But the trouble is with our pride. We spend so much of our time feeling like God that we're unwilling to confess and admit that we have failed. We get into all sorts of trouble trying to hide our sins and failures. We wear masks. We repress. We rationalize. We project or blame others, when the easiest thing to do would be to admit, "Yes, I'm human. I have failed. I have fallen, but I will not stay fallen. Like the prodigal son, I will arise and go to my father and say, 'Father, I have sinned. . . .' "

Secondly, failure can be our greatest teacher. I like what William A. Ward said once, "Failure should be our *teacher*, *not our undertaker*. It should challenge us to new heights of accomplishment, not pull us to new depths of despair. Failure is delay but not *defeat*. It is a temporary detour, not a dead-end street."

It has been said that life is like playing basketball. We make very few direct hits into the basket. It's our ability to make the rebounds that counts. In fact, the team with the most rebounds usually wins the game.

I heard a scientist say once that science learns more from its failures than from its successes. If an experiment is successful, science discovers a *theory* which is probably true. But if an experiment is not successful, if it fails, then science discovers a *fact*, i.e., something that is definitely not true.

A young assistant to Thomas A. Edison said once, "Mr. Edison, we have performed the same experiment 800 times and we have failed each time. Why don't we give up?" Mr. Edison replied, "We have not failed. We have discovered 800 ways it will not work."

Bobby Jones, the great golf champion, said, "I never learned anything from the games I won. All I know about golf I learned from the matches I lost."

Man has had to perform many experiments and often fail, in order to make progress. His progress has come through failure. Thus, failure, far from being an undertaker, has been a great teacher to man. It has helped man grow. It has helped him to develop judgment and become mature. It has shown man his weaknesses. It has taught him that he is not sufficient of himself. It has pointed him to a source of power in Christ which is inexhaustible. Thus, instead of fretting when we meet failure, we would do well to ask ourselves, "What great lesson is God trying to teach me through this failure?" The prodigal son's failure taught him the great lesson that true happiness and freedom are to be found not in the far country of sin but with God.

We have said thus far that it is human to fail and that some of life's greatest blessings come out of temporary failure. This brings us to our third and last point: failure need not be the end of the road. It can be the beginning of a new and more beautiful journey.

Few people perhaps failed more than Abraham Lincoln. In 1832 he lost his job.

In 1832 he was defeated in his campaign for the legislature.

In 1833 he failed in business.

In 1835 his sweetheart died.

In 1835 he failed in the Black Hawk War.

In 1838 he was defeated as Speaker for the House.

In 1843 he was defeated in his bid for nomination to Congress.

In 1848 he lost the renomination for Congress.

In 1849 he was rejected as a land officer.

In 1854 he was defeated for the Senate.

In 1856 he was defeated for the nomination to the Vice Presidency.

In 1858 he was defeated again in his bid for the Senate.

But in 1860 he was elected President of the United States!

One biographer said of Lincoln, "He fell 17 times in the course of his life but each time he fell in the direction of the White House."

Judas fell but he chose to remain fallen. That was real failure. Peter fell. Three times he denied his Lord. But he did not stay fallen. And Jesus said to him, "Thou art Peter and on this rock I will build my church." The prodigal son fell but he chose to rise again. "I will arise and go to my father." Thank God, we, too, have a Father who is all-merciful and will receive us as joyfully as the prodigal son was received by his father.

The pagan Greek philosopher Celsus said once, "Every other teacher summons to him the best people, the clever and the good, but this crazy Jesus calls to him the beaten and the broken, the ragtag and the bobtail, the failures and the scum." But far from being shamed by this, the Church was proud of it. "Yes, it's true," they said, "Christ does take the broken and the defeated, but He doesn't leave them broken and defeated. Out of the failures you would throw away, He makes new men, gives them another chance."

In the book entitled *Jesus: A Dialogue with the Saviour*, written by a monk of the Eastern Church, the author pictures Jesus addressing to him the merciful call, "Follow thou Me."

And the monk answers,

"Master, I have so often and for so many years heard the call! How many times I have started on the way! And then I have fallen, I have not continued. I have gotten up again; I have fallen again. I cannot say that I have followed You. I have lost sight of You, and yet I have always felt that You were there. . . .

"Get up again. Begin again. But then, You mean, Master, I am not rejected in spite of my innumerable betrayals?"

"Come after Me. Follow Me."

In 1666 the great fire of London raged for five days and five nights destroying the old Gothic Cathedral of St. Paul. Only one single massive column stood after the fire, and amazingly enough it bore the motto: "I shall rise again." May that be the motto of our life always, "No matter how many times I fall, 'I will arise and go to my Father.' "

I close with these words by St. John Climacus.

"It is the property of angels not to fall, and even, as some say, it is quite impossible for them to fall. It is the property of men to fall and to rise again as often as this may happen. But it is the property of devils, and devils alone, not to rise once they have fallen."

Chapter Twenty-Nine

"WHO SINNED?"

WHEN EDWARD SHELDON, the famous American playwright, became afflicted with arthritis which permanently crippled him, and eventually robbed him of his sight as well, he said: "If I only knew what I have ever done to bring this upon me!"

The same question was asked by the disciples in John 9:2 when they saw the lad who had been born blind: "Master, who sinned, this man, or his parents, that he was born blind?" To them it was inconceivable that anyone should be so tragically handicapped unless either he or his parents had sinned grievously. To them suffering was punishment for sin.

Don't we reflect this same attitude in our feelings today? Don't we, too, feel that there is a direct relationship between sin and suffering? Don't we feel that if we are truly faithful to God we will be immune from suffering and hurts? How often do we say when suffering befalls us, "I am a man of faith; why did this happen to me? I pray; why did this come to my family? I am a good church member; why should I be haunted by failure and disease?" But the assumption is wrong and dangerous. Suffering is *not* always a form of punishment. Sometimes it may be, as in the case of the alcoholic who drinks himself into a sickness, *but not always*.

The Book of Job in the Old Testament was written to show us that suffering is not necessarily punishment for personal wrongdoing. Job, though he suffered so deeply, was an innocent man. It might have been supposed that thereafter this view would no longer be held. But apparently it still was current in the day of Jesus as we read in the Gospel:

"As Jesus passed by, he saw a man blind from birth. And his disciples asked him, 'Master, who sinned, this man, or his parents, that he was born blind?' Jesus answered, *'Neither has this man sinned, nor his parents: but that the works of God might be made manifest in him.' "*

It might have been supposed that after the Lord Jesus himself had condemned this view so strongly, it would have died a natural death. But it seems to have lingered on even down to the present day. Dr. Paul Tournier, psychiatrist, writes, *"Countless despairing people have had to undergo indescribable suffering and torture of mind simply because their ills have been thought to be the result of their actual sins."* Another person—one of the leading counselors in our country—says this: *"No matter how intellectual we may become, when suffering overtakes us we feel that God has forsaken us, or more specifically that He is actually punishing us."*

And yet God himself tells us that suffering has no necessary relation to sin. A man may suffer deeply without in any way deserving to do so. After all, what did Jesus do to deserve the cross? He was without sin and yet He suffered—suffered greatly. How then can anyone say that suffering is always the result of personal sin?

At another time Jesus told of a tower which toppled over and killed 18 persons. Everyone thought the victims must have done something evil for which they were now punished by God. But Jesus explained that those 18 persons were not any worse than other sinners: *". . . those eighteen upon whom the tower in Siloam fell, and killed them, do you think they were worse offenders than all the others that dwelt in Jerusalem? I tell you, No: but unless you repent, you will all likewise perish"* (Luke 13:2–5).

Who, then, can ever say of another person that his sickness or suffering is punishment by God for some sin? "Let him who is without sin cast the first stone," said Jesus. Are we not all sinners? Many times we hear people say, "Why does God allow the tyrants and the great tormentors of humanity to exist?" "Why doesn't He strike them dead?" But as Dorothy Sayers, the detective writer, says, "Why, madam, did He not strike you dumb before you uttered that baseless and unkind slander the day before yesterday? Or me, before I behaved with such cruel lack of consideration to that well-meaning friend? And why, sir, did he not cause your hand to rot off at the wrist before you signed your name to that dirty little bit of financial trickery?" We cannot always lay the blame for suffering at the door of sin. We are all sinful, every one of us.

But Jesus went on to say that even though the young lad was not blind because of sin, his suffering had meaning: "Neither hath this man sinned, nor his parents; *but that the works of God should be made manifest in him.*" Suffering always has meaning to those who have committed their life to God. "All things work together for good to those who love God," wrote St. Paul. God can do some things with you, if your life is committed to Him, that He can't do if you just run to Him when you're in trouble. God can't work with anybody and everybody for their good. They won't let Him! They won't commit their lives to Him. But if you do love Him, if you are really trying to line up your life with His will, then He can work with you, in any event at all, for your deepest and truest good and "the works of God will be made manifest in your life." His love and power will shine forth in all their splendor even in your suffering.

For one thing we see things in sorrow and suffering that we never saw before. A few summers ago a young man fell overboard in the Hawaiian yacht races. For thirty hours he floated alone in shark-infested waters. When he was rescued, the reporters say that he had a strange look on his face, as if he had been in another world. When they asked him what he had thought about all that time while he was floating so near to sudden death; his answer was: "I thought about the time, all the time, I had wasted in my life."

There is a little poem which expresses it this way:

> "I walked a mile with Pleasure,
> She chatted by the way,
> But left me none the wiser
> For all she had to say.
> I walked a mile with Sorrow,
> And ne'er a word spake she.
> But oh! The things I learned from her
> When sorrow walked with me."

The veteran actor William Gargan related in *Guideposts* magazine how he found the answer to a torturing question.

He writes: "There's a question that, sooner or later, all of us seem to ask. When trouble comes or sickness or heartache, our hands go out in a gesture of bewilderment and we ask: 'WHY ME?' Or perhaps you've heard it as 'What have I done to deserve this?' Or 'Why pick on me?'

"Two years ago it was my turn to complain to God in just those words: 'WHY ME?' And yet I could phrase them only in my mind. I lay in a hospital unable to talk. The only way I could communicate words was to write them. My larynx, or voice box, had been removed because of cancer, and I lay there in deep depression. Here I was an actor who could not speak. It was like being an athlete who could not run or a painter who could not see. For 35 years I'd been in the entertainment world, in movies, radio, stage, TV. Suddenly it was all over."

He goes on to say that the operation had been a success. The cancer had been removed. Before the operation he prayed as he always had, and he received strength. He had not feared dying but now—after surgery—he was afraid to live knowing that he would never be able to speak again.

"WHY ME, GOD?" he asked again with lip that brought forth no sound. "Are you punishing me for something I've done wrong?"

Finally, doctors told him of a way by which he could learn to speak again—not as well as before—but it would be speech. Esophageal speech, they called it. With much discipline, effort and help from others who had the same operation and used esophageal speech, he managed to learn to speak again. After that, he was in constant demand all over the country as a speaker before "Lost Chord" clubs and other groups of people who had lost their speech because of this same surgery. His example encouraged thousands of laryngectomees to learn to speak again.

He concludes the article by saying:

"I believe that God is forever creating such opportunities for us, but often we are too involved in ourselves to grasp them. That's why the next time I'm inclined to complain with a petulant 'WHY ME?' I'll change it quickly to 'WHY NOT ME, GOD?' " *

"Neither has this man sinned, nor his parents; but that the works of God might be made manifest in him."

---

* Copyright 1963, Guideposts Associates, Inc., Carmel, New York.

Chapter Thirty

WHEN WE HAVE DONE ALL WE CAN
— THEN WHAT?

ART LINKLETTER HAS SHOWN that some of the funniest and yet most thought-provoking words come out of the mouths of babes. The following story confirms his findings.

A little four-year-old girl was told to pray for her absent father, her small brother who was ill, and a friend who had sprained an ankle. She did so and to the mother's surprise concluded the prayer as follows: "And now, God, please take good care of yourself, for if anything ever happens to You we'll all be in the soup."

The Gospel of Matthew (15:22) tells of a mother who came to Jesus with a prayer that He heal her sick daughter. There was nothing else she could do. There was simply no one who could heal her daughter. She could have given up hope and said, "What's the use? There is no God in this world—at least not a God who cares." But her faith was too great to allow her to be overcome by discouragement. She came to Jesus and prayed, "Have mercy on me, O Lord, Son of David; my daughter is severely possessed of a demon."

Sometimes there is nothing we can do but pray. I remember something General Dwight Eisenhower said once. One night in July of 1943 he watched a vast armada of 3,000 ships sailing from Malta to the shore of Sicily for a great invasion. The General saluted his heroic men and then bowed his head in prayer. To an officer beside him, Eisenhower explained, "There comes a time when you've used all your brains, all your training, all your technical skill, and the die is cast. The events are in the hands of God and there you have to leave them."

Judge Harold Medina, who presided at the trial of eleven communist leaders in 1949, tells how during the trial he came to a point where he was beaten. His nerves were frayed by telephone calls and threats against his life and the lives of members of his family. He said, "One day I felt I *had* to leave the courtroom. And, I'll be frank about it, when I left I was certain I could never go back. I had stood as much as as I could. I had to give up.

"But suddenly there in my room I found myself like a frightened child calling to his father in the dark. I asked God to take charge of things and that His will be done. I cannot report anything mysterious or supernatural. All I know is that as I lay on the couch some new kind of strength flowed into me. That brief period of communion with my Maker saved not only the trial but my sanity as well."

So there are times when we have done all we can and there is nothing else we can do but pray—times when, instead of tightening up with tension, we "LET GO AND LET GOD" as the expression goes. We relax, place all our trust in God and let Him take over.

Guideposts magazine has two stories that illustrate this. One tells of a young Navy lieutenant who was part of an underwater demolition team. He became involved in an auto accident in France and lay near death in a hospital. As a Navy "frogman" he had learned to break one fatigue barrier with another. He was in top physical shape. But on the hospital bed he realized that his own will and determination were of no help to him. In his *complete helplessness* he turned to God in prayer. This is how he describes what happened:

"I lay there on my bed, closed my eyes and with my mind tried to reach up to God. My prayer was an admission of my helplessness and a willingness to believe in His greatness. It was a sort of 'You can—I can't' prayer.

"From that moment things were different. I felt different. The doctors almost immediately noted a change for the better in my condition. At a point when all my will power and determination had no effect whatsoever on my burns, God answered my call and combined the skill of the surgeons with the healing balm of His love.

"Today, two years later, I have my vision back, I walk as well as before, I have good use of my right hand and some of my left. Last May I married the wonderful girl who waited so patiently for me.

"I have much to be thankful for—most of all a new closeness to God who showed me that *when man reaches the end of his resources, God's love and power are there to help him achieve a new breakthrough.*"

In the same issue of *Guideposts* a woman, Jane Britt of Minneapolis, writes:

"Several years ago I reached the point of deep despair and I checked into a hospital, mainly to rest. I had just lost my husband, from cancer, after a year's gallant fight on his part and the part of doctors. My grief at times seemed to engulf me completely, rushing over me, filling my being with utter loneliness and deep, deep sorrow.

"The day after arriving I went down to the hospital chapel, slipped into one of the pews, dropped to my knees—and tried to pray. Words would not come easily, and finally I did not try anymore. I just knelt there in the silence of the little chapel.

"After a while I arose and slowly walked back to my room. Inside, my eyes fell on a letter which had been delivered in my absence. I tore open the envelope. It was a condolence note from my friend Wilma who wrote that the following words by Grace Noll Crowell said everything she wanted to say to me:

FOR ONE WHO IS TIRED

Dear child, God does not say today, "Be strong,"
He knows your strength is spent, He knows how long
The road has been, how weary you have grown,
For He who walked the earthly roads along
Each boggy lowland and each rugged hill,
Can understand, and so He says, "Be still,
And know that I am God." The hour is late
And you must rest awhile, and you must wait
Until life's empty reservoirs fill up,
As slow rain fills an empty upturned cup.
Hold up your cup, dear child, for God to fill;
He only asks today that you be still.*

---

* Crowell, Grace Noll, *Songs of Hope* (Harper and Brothers, copyright 1938). Reprinted by permission of Harper and Row, publishers.

"How I needed those words at that very moment! And in the days that followed God did indeed fill my empty cup." *

Andre Maurois in his book *Why France Fell* tells of a conversation he had once with the late Winston Churchill. Maurois asked him why during the beginning of the Second World War, England seemed so unwilling to fight. Churchill turned to Maurois and said, "Have you observed the habits of lobsters?" "No," said Maurois. Churchill went on, "Well, if you have the opportunity, study them. At certain periods in its life the lobster loses its protective shell. At this moment even the bravest lobster retires into a crevice in a rock, and waits patiently until a new shell has time to grow. As soon as this new armor has grown strong, he sallies forth out of the crevice, and becomes once more a fighter, lord of the seas." England— said Churchill—had lost its shell and had to wait for a new one to grow.

There are times when we, too, lose our protective shell. Like Judge Medina, like the young Navy lieutenant, like Jane Britt, the widow from Minneapols, we come to the end of our rope. We find ourselves completely helpless. Then, like the lobster, we too can retire into the crevice of our Rock who is God and there through prayer we wait upon the Lord to fill our empty cup with new strength. "They who wait upon the Lord," says the prophet Isaiah, "shall renew their strength, they shall mount up with wings like eagles, they shall run and not be weary, they shall walk and not faint" (Isa. 40:31).

So there are times when we have done all we can and there is nothing else we can do but LET GO AND LET GOD take over.

"Have mercy on me, O Lord. Son of David; my daughter is severely possessed of a demon." And Jesus said, "O woman. great is your faith! Be it done for you as you desire."

---

*Both stories used by permission. Copyright 1965 Guideposts Associates, Inc., Carmel, N.Y.

Chapter Thirty-One

HE HAS NO HANDS BUT OURS!

SOMEONE ONCE SAID that nature is very wise. In making a man's body, the hands were placed in front to make it extremely awkward for man to pat himself on the back. Yet man somehow manages to overcome the limitations of nature—this one included.

Hands make a fascinating study. Of all the members of our body perhaps the hands are the most marvelous. Man does not have an eye as sharp as the eagle's. He does not have a nose as keen as the dog's. He does not have an ear as alert as the horse. And he does not have a sense of touch as sensitive as the spider's, but man outclasses all the lower creatures with his hands. Not even the ape can claim to have the amazing dexterity of man's hands.

There are even people who claim to be able to tell the fortunes or misfortunes of life by studying the palm of the hand. Of course, we do not place much faith in such soothsayers. But there is a sense in which your hands reveal the real you. Hands may sometimes tell your character. Often they offer a hint as to your vocation. And they can even reveal what kind of a Christian you are.

Consider how much the hands of Jesus tell us about Him. There was the leper who came to Him. St. Mark captured the action of the moment. "Jesus," he writes, "moved with compassion, *put forth his hand*, and touched him." The law of the day stated that no one was to touch a leper for fear of infection. Jesus touched him and healed him. A distraught father, Jairus, came to Him one day crying, "Master, my daughter has just died but come and lay your hands on her, and she will live." He touched her and brought her back to life. With His hands Jesus blessed children. With His hands He washed the feet of His disciples. When He appeared in the upper room following the resurrection, He showed the disciples His pierced hands and they believed. "Such mighty works are wrought by his hands," writes St. Mark.

At the end of the last war a platoon of American soldiers came to a bombed-out church. They found a statue of Christ that was smashed. They collected most of the pieces and cemented them together—all but the hands. These could not be found anywhere. Finally one soldier made a sign and left it by the partially restored statue of Christ. The sign read, "He has no hands but yours."

Perhaps inspired by this statue, Annie Johnson Flint wrote the following poem:

"Christ has no hands but our hands
    To do His work today;
He has no feet but our feet
    To lead men in His way;
He has no tongue but our tongues
    To tell men how He died;
He has no help but our help
    To bring them to His side."

You may have heard the legend—and it is only a legend—of how Christ returned to heaven following His resurrection, still bearing the marks of His sufferings. One of the angels asked Him, "You must have suffered terribly for men down there." "I did," said Jesus. "Do they all know about what you did for them," asked the angel. "No," said Jesus, "not yet. So far only a few know about it in Palestine." "And," asked the angel, "have you made plans so that they may all come to know about it?" "Well," said Jesus, "I asked my apostles to make it their business to tell others, and the others still others, until the entire world comes to know about it." With a look of horror, the angel said, "Yes, but your apostles failed you so often. What if they should fail to tell the story of your love! What then? Haven't you made any other plans?" And back came the answer of Jesus, "I haven't made any other plans. I am counting on them."

Christ has chosen to work through us. He has no hands but

ours. As St. Augustine said, "Without God, we cannot. Without us, God will not."

When you were baptized and confirmed, the sign of the cross was made on your hands and the other members of your body with the holy oil of Chrismation. By this act your hands were dedicated to the service of Christ. They became members of the Body of Christ. If the Church is called the Body of Christ, it is because it is exactly that—the body through which Christ works in the world today. By baptism we become members of the Church, i.e., the Body of Christ. This means that after baptism our hands are Christ's hands. They are the hands by which Christ must work in the world today. St. Chrysostom said once, "Christ is the Head of the Body, but of what use is the head without eyes, without ears, without feet, without hands?" "Now you are the body of Christ and individually members of it" (I Cor. 12:27).

Dr. Carl Jung said once, "Man is indispensable for the completion of creation: he himself is the second creator of the world...." God has placed man in an incomplete and imperfect world. He has placed him here as a second creator to complete the work of creation. A man once cleared away a terrible patch of weeds and created a beautiful garden. A passing tourist saw the beautiful garden and said, "It's wonderful what God can do with a bit of ground like this, isn't it?" "Yes," said the man who had sweated to remove the weeds, "but you should have seen this bit of ground when God had it by himself!" If God is to create gardens out of the patches of weeds in this world, He must use our hands.

A cripple once fell and lay helpless in the Louvre at the feet of Venus de Milo. As he lay there, he said, "The blessed Goddess of Beauty, our Dear Lady of Milo, looked down on me with mingled compassion and desolation, seeming to say, 'Do you not see that I have no arms, and therefore cannot help you?' "

Venus of Milo may have no hands, but Christ has. The hands of every Christian in the world today are His hands. But, alas, many of these hands are as withered as were the hands of the person in the Gospels who came to Jesus for healing. They are withered by inactivity and unconcern.

"There's somebody near you who's lost on the way,
   Struggling, bewildered, alone;
Somebody who's tired and weary, to whom
   The love of the Lord should be shown;
Reach him a helping hand."

That is what we *should* be doing: reaching a helping hand.
But the saddest things about the hands of many Christians today is that they are *withered*.

A disgusted detective said once, "This was the perfect crime.
The criminal never left a fingerprint anywhere." Commenting
on this Halford Luccock wrote, "Isn't that the perfect crime
against life? Not to leave a fingerprint anywhere? Not to touch
any life or institution or cause with a personal touch that
leaves a mark upon it? Some people can go through life with
gloves on, never really touching anything. Others, thank God,
leave the mark of a great love on the people and the enterprises
they touch."

There are *withered* hands. There are also hands like Pilate's
—constantly washing themselves of any responsibility. These
are the people who say, "I don't like this racial discrimination.
But what can I do? It isn't my fault. My hands are clean."
Even today Pilate's washbowl is being passed around.

There are *withered* hands. There are *washed* hands. There
are *empty* hands. After a great earthquake in Tokyo many
years ago no one was admitted into the city unless he came
bearing rice and a candle. In a city of so much suffering there
was no room for empty hands. There never is. Not in this world.
Not if ours are the hands of Christ.

Withered hands, brought to Christ, are made whole. When
Jesus saw the man with the withered hand, He said, "Stretch
out your hand." And He restored it to wholeness.

One of the fascinating stories found in the Bible concerns
a little boy who had a few sandwiches and some fish. He could
have eaten this lunch and been entirely forgotten, but he is
remembered through the centuries. He didn't have much in
his hand, but what he had he willingly gave to the Lord. The
Lord took what was in the hands of the little boy and multiplied
it a thousandfold, creating enough food to feed five thousand
people.

What do you have in your hand? It may not be much more than the few sandwiches that little boy had; but the secret is to turn it over to the Lord, to let Him use it. He will multiply it a thousandfold and use it to bring blessing to many.

The hands of a Christian are praying hands. It is through prayer that they develop muscle-tone and power for the tasks of the day. We recall the famous prayer of Moses when he prayed for Israel until his upraised hands became weary and had to be supported by Hur and Aaron. Christian hands do not stop with prayer. They begin with prayer. They go on from prayer to work. They try to become part of the answer to prayer.

A poor man who lived in the country broke his leg. He was laid up for a long time, unable to work. His family was large and needed help. Someone got up a prayer meeting at the church to pray for this man. While people were asking God to help the family there was a loud knock on the door. Opening the door, they found a young farm boy who said, "My dad could not attend the prayer meeting tonight so he just sent his prayer in a wagon." And there was the wagon loaded with meat, potatoes, apples, and other things from the farm. Praying hands are hands that are willing to work, to load their prayers in a wagon, to become part of the answer to prayer.

Dr. Louis Evans visited a mission field in Korea and spent some time with a missionary doctor, a man who had left a lucrative practice at home to follow the call of Christ. One day he watched as the doctor performed a long and arduous operation lasting over seven hours in a stifling little room. "Is every day like this?" he asked the surgeon when it was over. The surgeon only smiled. Beads of perspiration stood out on his forehead, his lips were purple with strain, his hands trembled with fatigue. "How much would you get paid for an operation like this back in America?" asked Evans. "About 500 dollars," came the reply. "It was a complicated one." "How much will you get here?" The surgeon turned and looked at the poor Korean woman. She had been wheeled into the operating room clutching only a copper coin and begging him in Christ's name to give her back her life. With a smile spreading across his tired face, he said, "For this I will get her gratitude and my

Master's smile. And that, sir, is worth more than all the praise and money that the world could give." The hands of that surgeon were the hands of Christ continuing in the world today the work of caring, healing, loving.

One of the most moving scenes in English literature comes at the end of Dickens' *Tale of Two Cities*. The carts were rumbling through the thronged streets of Paris to the guillotine. In one of them were two prisoners: a brave man who was giving his life for a friend, and beside him a girl—little more than a child. She had seen him in prison and had observed the gentleness and courage in his face. "If I may ride with you," she had asked, thinking of that last dread journey, "will you let me hold your hand? I am not afraid, but I am little and weak, and it will give me courage." They rode together, her hand in his; and even when they reached the place of execution, there was no fear at all in her eyes. She looked at the quiet, composed face of the man beside her and said, "I think you were sent to me by heaven." He was. His hands were the strengthening hands of Christ.

God is looking for hands to use. Even today He carries the cross—the cross of love, of concern for those who live in darkness, for the sinner, for the poor, the afflicted, the maligned, the deprived, the downtrodden. He looks to us, to our hands, to help Him lift that cross.

Dr. Reuben Youngdahl tells of a group of natives in East Africa who made a long journey to seek medical care. They walked right past a government hospital to reach a mission hospital. When asked why they had walked the extra distance, when the government hospital had exactly the same medicine, they replied, "The medicine may be the same, but *the hands are different*." The hands of a Christian are always different because they are the hands of Christ.

A woman once saw a statue of Christ on trial before Pilate. The Master's hands were tied behind His back. She looked at the statue and said, "If we could only untie His hands!" This is our task as Christians—to untie the hands of Christ by grasping our world with these: His hands of love.

"Take my hands and let them move,
At the impulse of Thy love."

Chapter Thirty-Two

CAN A MAN BE PERFECT?

NOT LONG AGO AN AD SHOWED a Volkswagen with a flat tire. The headline read, "Nobody's perfect."

How often we hear the excuse, "I'm not perfect, but then, who is?" It's an excuse we use to cover a multitude of sins.

Evidently the Lord Jesus had other ideas about the possibility of perfection. He says in Matthew 5:48, "You, therefore, must be perfect, as your heavenly Father is perfect."

There are those, of course, who feel that this ideal of perfection that Jesus holds up before us is impossible. It is unattainable, unrealistic, too high. It is a code for angels, not for men. One would have to be more than human to live up to it. So, like the Rich Young Ruler who came to see Jesus and found the demands of discipleship too exacting, they shake their heads and walk away.

But is it really an impossible goal? Does not man by nature strive for the highest and best? Is man ever satisfied with a machine he has made—a computer, for example? Does he not strive constantly to perfect it, to come out with a new and better model?

Theodore P. Ferris says, "If a boy is interested in baseball and wants to be a good baseball player, whom does he want to be like? One of the players on the local team? Not at all. He wants to be like Babe Ruth and Ted Williams. In other words, he reaches for the stars." Man by nature reaches for the highest. It is as he sets challenging goals; it is as he reaches for the stars that he makes progress.

If Jesus calls us to perfection, then it is because He believes it is possible to attain this ideal. He believes that sinners can become saints. He believes that moral pygmies, such as we are, can become giants. "You, therefore, must be perfect as your heavenly Father is perfect." "It is indeed a code for angels," says A. Leonard Griffith, "but Jesus believed with the Psalmist that we humans are just 'a little lower than angels.'" If Jesus challenges us with nothing short of perfection it is because He believes there is something great in us.

And that which is great in each one of us is the image of God. The Greek Fathers distinguish between the terms IMAGE and LIKENESS. Man, they say, was made in the *image* of God but not in the *likeness* of God. Because we are made in the image of God we have a mind and free will; we can know God and have communion with Him. If man makes proper use of this faculty for communion with God, he will progress toward the goal of divine likeness: "You, therefore, must be perfect." This accounts for the great emphasis the Greek Fathers place on the theosis of man, i.e., that man through Jesus Christ and by the grace of the Holy Spirit can be lifted out of the life of fallen humanity into the very life of God. He can become transfigured, deified. As Dr. Nikos Nissiotis writes, "The theosis of which the Orthodox speak . . . is that spiritual ascension worked in us by the Paraclete . . . *which leads us to true and complete humanity.*" *

The command to perfection, then, is really a command to grow from image to likeness and to keep growing. The only way to approach this command toward perfection is by growth. We are certainly not going to achieve perfection all at once. We are to pursue it, so that we may grow toward it.

Robert Frost, the poet, wrote:

"The woods are lovely, dark and deep,
But I have promises to keep,
And miles to go before I sleep."

How well these words express the truth that we were not made to stand still. We were made to keep moving, to keep growing, to seek perfection. There are times when we shall succeed and times when we shall fail, but by God's grace we shall learn from both our successes and our failures and we shall make them steppingstones to higher achievement.

A teacher told once of a youngster who, on his first day at

---

* *The Orthodox Ethos,* Vol. I, p. 59. Edited by A. J. Philippou.

kindergarten, wandered around examining the low tables and chairs. Everything was just the right size for a five-year-old. Finally, he walked up to the teacher and said, "I don't like it here. There is nothing to grow up to." Jesus saw to it that we shall always have something to grow up to. "You, therefore, must be perfect, as your heavenly Father is perfect."

When Jesus said, "You must be perfect," He did not say perfect "like your friends, perfect like Tom, Dick and Harry." He said, "You must be perfect as your heavenly Father is perfect." In other words, there is such a thing as a standard of perfection.

A violin teacher was asked one day, "Well, what's the good news?" The old music teacher walked over to the tuning fork and struck it with a mallet. "There is the good news for today," he said. "That, my friend, is A. It was A all day yesterday. It will be A all day tomorrow, next week, and for a thousand years. The soprano upstairs warbles off-key, the tenor next door flats his high ones, and the piano across the hall is out of tune. Noise all around me, noise; but that, my friend, is A."

We have the same noise all around us today—the noise of the moral confusion of the day, but thank God, He has sounded the note A; He has given us the standard of perfection: "You, therefore, must be perfect *as your heavenly Father* is perfect."

A short time ago an article appeared in one of our national magazines entitled, "Let's Stop Exalting Punks." The article stated that our moral values are fading because of the kind of heroes we hold up before our young people. A week's admiration for men like astronauts Gus Grissom and John Young hardly makes up for 51 weeks of admiration for men without honor. I guess the ancient Greeks were wiser than we are. They chose for their heroes half-gods. Jesus was even wiser than the ancient Greeks. He chose for our hero One who is entirely worthy of emulation. "You, therefore, must be perfect, as your heavenly Father is perfect."

But how, you object, can we set about imitating the perfections of Almighty God? He is eternal; are we to imitate Him in that? He is omniscient; are we to imitate Him in that?

He is all-powerful; are we to imitate Him in that? And how are we to imitate our heavenly Father when we have never seen Him?

This is a real difficulty and it was raised by Philip over 1900 years ago. "Lord, show us the Father," said Philip, "and we shall be satisfied." Jesus replied, "Have I been so long a time with you, and yet you do not know me, Philip? He who has seen me has seen the Father; how can you say, 'Show us the Father?' " (John 14:8, 9). This, then, is the answer to our difficulty. We have seen the goodness and the perfection of the Father. Through the Incarnation it was translated into a language we can understand: a human life, the perfect life of Jesus. He who sees Jesus sees two things: he sees God the Father and he sees also himself as God wills him to be. Jesus is qualified to serve as our model since He was completely human as we are. He was not immune from the frailties, the doubts, the temptations of human nature. Many times we try to make of Jesus a sort of superman. We overemphasize His divine nature. But do we not do this in an attempt to increase the breach between ourselves and Him, to protect ourselves from any obligation to be like Him? Lecomte du Nouy, the French physicist, wrote once, "The perfect man is not a myth: he has lived in Jesus Christ." St. Gregory of Nazianzen writes that "Jesus represents the archetype of what we are and can become."

In Jesus Christ, then, God has shown us the pattern from which we are made. He has shown us the only kind of life in which we can find our highest fulfillment and completion as persons.

The great French Christian, Fenelon, said once, "A peasant shut up in his village only partially knows his wretchedness, but let him see rich palaces, a superb court, and he will realize all the poverty of his village. He cannot endure the hovels after a sight of such magnificence." Perhaps this is one of the reasons God lived with us in this world in the person of Christ: to make us feel dissatisfied with ourselves until we have captured something of the grandeur of Christ.

But lest I leave you with a false impression let me try to clarify something. Don't think for a moment that we have to be perfect before God will accept us. We do not have to win God's favor by doing things perfectly. God accepts us as we are—sinners. But He wants us to become more than we now are. He wants us to grow, to pattern our lives after Christ.

The second false impression I want to erase is that to be a Christian one must be a *perfectionist*. A perfectionist, I think, is a sick person. He misses the joy of life because he thinks he must be perfect in everything. He cannot accept failure. He has not yet realized that it is human to fail, that we learn some of our greatest lessons from our failures.

I am reminded here of the legendary Indian princess. She went to a neighboring chief whose cornfields were the talk of all the tribes. She asked if she might select one ear for seed. He granted her permission to walk down the longest row and take the finest ear she could find. He made only one condition. She must choose as she walked down the row; she could not turn back and pluck an ear she had once passed. The princess, of course, kept looking for the perfect ear until she walked right out of the cornfield empty-handed. She was too much of a perfectionist.

Perhaps the Church seems to be *perfectionistic* at times, especially when she sets before us the perfect life of Christ and says, "There you are. That's the true life! That's the way to live!" If that is the Gospel, then it is a Gospel of despair. Who can fully live the life of Christ?

If after hearing Isaac Stern play the violin, someone were to hand you a violin and say, "Here. Now you saw how it is done. I want you to play like that." You would say, "Impossible. I'm not Isaac Stern. And besides I don't know the first thing about a violin."

So it is with Christ. If He were only an example, it would be impossible to imitate Him. But Jesus is not first an example: first He is Lord and Saviour, then He becomes example. If we accept Him as Lord and Saviour and live in close relationship with Him, He will send the Holy Spirit to live in us and give us the power to live the life of Christ. This is comparable to having Isaac Stern come to live in us and play through us. Then we would really hear music! The fulfillment of the command to perfection becomes possible only after we have received the Holy Spirit within us.

The end product of the command, "You, therefore, must be perfect . . ." is that Christ will become incarnate in us. One day a Yale graduate took his son to his alma mater to enroll him. He told the dean of students his dream for the boy, "I want him to get exactly what I got when I was here." The dean asked, "You mean you want him to follow in your footsteps." The father smilingly agreed. The dean said, "Look, now! You're a great guy and we're proud of you, but don't you think one of you is enough?"

One of Christ is never enough for this world. He must live in each Christian so that there is not one but millions of Christs in the world today. We bear His name, why not His life? why not His love? Our emphasis should be not so much on what Christ can do for us but on what we can do for Christ in the world by being to some slight degree like Him.

Someone said to the widow of Dr. Edward Wilson who perished on Scott's expedition to the Antarctic, "I never thought the Christ-life was possible as an ideal until I saw it in your husband." When we see Christ living in His followers, the command, "You must be perfect . . ." becomes no longer an impossible ideal but the highest, the noblest, the worthiest, most challenging goal toward which a man `can strive in this life.

On the gravestone of an Alpine mountain climber are engraved the words, *He died climbing.* What nobler thing can be said of any Christian when the end comes than, "He died climbing toward the high calling of God in Christ Jesus."

Chapter Thirty-Three

"GOD, YOU TAKE THE NIGHT SHIFT"

SOMEONE SAID ONCE, "If we don't worry, we'll go to the poorhouse; if we do worry, we'll go to the insane asylum."

Living is so complicated these days that most of us don't even worry right. For instance,

> We worry about the Russians, then get run over by the neighbor's car.
>
> We worry about radio-active fallout, then get poisoned by nicotine.
>
> We worry about crashing in an airplane, then fall off the ladder painting the house.
>
> We worry about getting enough exercise, then drive two blocks for a cup of coffee.

It's not easy to worry properly. Many people worry themselves to death. So let's consider briefly the best way to worry.

Worry or anxiety is not all bad. Sometimes it helps us get things done. If we didn't worry a little about people and circumstances and things we have to do, we wouldn't get much done. Dr. Hastings, chief of psychiatry at the University of Minnesota, said once, "Anxiety is a healthy phenomenon. It is the motivating factor by which we get things done."

It's good, for example, to worry about the condition of your soul and where you will spend eternity. "What shall it profit a man if he gain the whole world and lose his soul?" asked Jesus. Sometimes we're anxious about the wrong things. Jesus tells us that there is one thing we should all be anxious about: our soul. Such anxiety will lead us to live in Christ and for Christ.

Worry is a normal part of life but it can easily become abnormal. Then it overpowers us. Then we become its victims. It saps our energy. It distorts our world. It fills us with fear. It paralyzes action. It leads to all kinds of illnesses both physical and mental. Dr. Mayo said once, "We have doubled the number of insane in thirty years. Insanity is a curious result of civilization. There are few insane among primitive races. The moment a man begins to worry he imperils his mind."

What leads a person to such excessive, abnormal worry?

First, a person worries excessively when he plays God. People can actually behave as if they were God. This happens when they act as if everything depends on them. A person said once that sometimes his worries piled up so high that he thought he would break under the strain. A friend replied, "That will never happen if you carry only your share, and don't try to take God's work out of His hands." Much of our excessive worry comes when we try to take God's work out of His hands; we act as if everything depends on us.

Secondly, excessive worry is caused by practical atheism, i.e., by acting as if there were no God. One day a great religious leader was extremely worried about a problem. Seeing him so despondent, his wife asked him if God had died.

"Why no," he said. "What makes you ask such a silly question?"

"Because," she said, "you're certainly acting as if He were dead, fretting and worrying the way you are." We need to remember that we are sons and daughters of a *living* God. We are God's children, not God's orphans.

A third cause of excessive worry is that small two-letter word "IF." What IF this should happen or what IF that should happen, what will happen to me?" We call this borrowing trouble from the future. The ancient Spartans had a cure for this kind of worrying. The Spartans, you recall, were a military people who believed in few words. Once when a feud was brewing between the Athenians and the Spartans, the Athenians sent a messenger to Sparta with this message, "If we come to your city we will burn it to the ground." The Spartans returned an answer composed of a single word, "IF."

A businessman in Des Moines kept a diary. At the end of each day he wrote in green ink the thing that worried him most about tomorrow. [TEN YEARS LATER HE CHECKED TO SEE IF THE THINGS HE WORRIED ABOUT MOST

HAD HAPPENED. HE FOUND THAT NOT ONE OF THEM
HAD EVER OCCURRED.]

A great cure for worry is found in the Gospel where the
Lord Jesus says, *"Consider the lilies of the field, how they grow;
they neither toil nor spin; yet I tell you, even Solomon in all
his glory was not arrayed like one of these. But if God so clothes
the grass of the field, which today is alive and tomorrow is
thrown into the oven, will he not much more clothe you, O men
of little faith?"*

Think of those words *"MUCH MORE"* and what they mean.
If God takes so much pain with a blade of grass, *how much
more* will He care for one of His own children? Elsewhere Jesus
says, "If you then who are evil know how to give good things
to your children, *how much more* will your heavenly Father
give good things to those who ask him." I like the words "HOW
MUCH MORE" because they express God's tremendous care
for us. The disease of anxious care and excessive worry is
born when we try to take God's place, when we act as if He
were dead, when we forget His infinite care for us.

Many Christians worry about the future of their children.
This is good concern, a healthy worry. All of us should have
such a worry, provided we don't let it become excessive. If we
have such a worry, we shall be motivated to bring our children
to church every Sunday where they will receive the inspiration
to live for Christ. We shall see to it that they receive the Sacraments regularly so that they may have power for life. We shall
be concerned as parents that our children attend Sunday school,
Vacation Church School, Summer Camp, retreats and other activities sponsored for youth by our church. We shall be concerned that we have an icon as a family altar at home and
that we practice family prayer. Having done all this we can
leave the rest to God. The answer to worry, then, is to do
what we can and let God take care of the rest.

An itinerant ranch hand applied for a job with only this
statement: "I can sleep when the wind blows." The prospective
employer was not sure about employing him, but being des-
perate for help, he decided to take him. One night a storm arose.
The owner called to his helper, but there was no reply. He
decided to check to see if everything was protected from the

wind storm. He found the windmill securely tied. The corral gate was adequately lashed. A tarpaulin was placed over the hay stack and staked to the ground. The owner went to the helper's quarters and found him fast asleep. Then he understood his recommendation: "I can sleep when the wind blows." He had done all he could, and now he could sleep in peace. It takes faith for us to do that with our problems. After doing all we can, we turn it over to God, and we relax and rest instead of worrying excessively.

A widow once had a rough go of it. She was left with twelve children. But she managed to do a splendid job. Someone asked her how she was able to do so well. She replied, "I entered into a partnership." "A partnership?" asked the friend. "Yes," replied the widow, "some years ago I entered into a partnership with God. I made a deal with Him. I said I would do the work if He would do the worrying. And I've gotten along well ever since."

Another person, a businessman, was worrying himself sick during World War II. One day he discovered the way out of his excessive worry. Each night as he prepared for bed, he knelt and prayed: "God, I've taken care of it the best I could all day; You take the night shift."

"Consider the lilies of the field, how they grow; they neither toil nor spin; yet I tell you, even Solomon in all his glory was not arrayed like one of these. But if God so clothes the grass of the field, which today is alive and tomorrow is thrown into the oven, will he not *much more* clothe you, O men of little faith?"

Chapter Thirty-Four

"JUDGE NOT!"

THERE WAS A PERSIAN YOUTH who would rise in the middle
of the night to pray and read the Koran. One night his father
awoke while he was reading. "Behold," the religious youth said
to his father, "your other children are lost in irreligious slum-
ber, while I alone awake to praise God." "Son of my soul,"
the wise father answered, "it is better to sleep than to awake
to talk about your brothers' faults!"

The Pharisee about whom Jesus speaks in the Gospels was a
religious man. He went to the temple to pray. Yet as he prayed,
he, too, criticized his brother's faults: "God, I thank thee that
I am not like other men, extortioners, unjust, adulterers, or
even like this publican, this tax collector."

Yet what did this Pharisee know of other people? What
did he know of this tax collector? How did he judge him? By
his rough garments? What did he know of the struggles that
publican had made to better himself? What do we know of
other people whom we judge? What do we know of their
hopes and dreams? Most of all, what do we know of their
struggles? And what do they know of us? How much we have
struggled and how much we have resisted?

An eminent psychiatrist says that what wears out a marriage, a family, and life in general is the spirit of judgment
which creeps in insidiously, unconsciously, unnoticed.

Concerning the spirit of judgment Jesus says, "Judge not"
(Matt. 7:1). And He proceeds to explain why we should not
judge others. First, He says we have *no authority* to do so. St.
Paul writes in Romans 14:4, "Who are you to pass judgment
on the servant of another? It is before his own master that
he stands or falls. And he will be upheld, for the Master is
able to make him stand." It is for the Master to judge the
servant, says Paul. You are not the Master; God is. So don't

dream of judging others, says Paul. But think of the account that you will have to give of yourself before God.

It is clear, then, that we judge our neighbor without authority to do so. But we also judge without *knowledge*. We do not know the man we judge. We cannot see his interior. We can never know all the facts about a man. We can never know all his motives, which may perhaps justify him.

Dr. Gilbert Wrenn, former educational psychologist at the University of Minnesota, said once, "In this matter of personal relationships, it is important that we understand not so much *what* a person does as *why* he does it." We judge on the basis of outward behavior. But this is not the most important factor in any instance. The important question is why a person does what he does. And most often we don't know this.

A man once flung a pail of water over Archelaos the Macedonian. Archelaos said nothing at all. He went about his business as calmly as before. When a friend asked him how he could bear it so serenely, Archelaos replied, "He threw the water not on me, but on the man he thought I was."

We judge without knowledge. Even if a person has committed a public crime, we do not know that he may not repent—or even that he has not already repented, and become one of those over whom the angels rejoice. Therefore, says Jesus, "Judge not."

There is an incident in Dostoevsky's *The Brothers Karamazov* where Alexi, disturbed by his father's behavior, tells his father that God will judge his deed. "Yes," replies the father, "but He will also understand me." Only God understands completely and knows us through and through. Only He can judge.

We judge without authority. We judge without knowledge. And, thirdly, we judge without love. Dr. Paul Tournier tells the following story:

"During our cruise to the North Cape last year I was leaning on the rail one day watching the wonderful Norwegian landscape slip by, with its incredibly green islands and shores contrasting with the great glaciers which come down almost to the sea. A doctor passed in silence, and stood against the same rail beside me, studying the same spectacle. After a moment or two he said, 'I'm quite upset. I have just been told that one of our colleagues here has been divorced and remarried. Is it true?' 'Yes,' I said. After a further silence, he went on, 'How is it possible? How can you agree to his taking his place among us Christian doctors?'

"I said nothing for the moment. Then my friend asked, 'Do you not believe that divorce is disobedience to God? a sin?' 'Certainly,' I said, 'but if we could have only sinless men among us, there would be no one here; at any rate, I should not be here. We are all alike, we are all forgiven sinners.' A long silence followed. My friend went away. Later he returned. 'You are right,' he said briefly, 'now I know what grace means.' " *

If we knew God's grace, God's forgiving love, we would hesitate to judge others. "Love is patient and kind; love is not jealous or boastful . . . it is not irritable or resentful." Love "does not rejoice at wrong, but rejoices in the right." God is the sole judge; yet even He judges in love. Archbishop William Temple said once, ". . . if you will think of God as first and foremost a Judge you will find Him a curious kind of Judge. He does indeed judge us. But He is not first Judge— He is first Father, and only judges as a Father judges."

An eminent artist was requested to paint the picture of Alexander the Great. He wanted to paint a perfect likeness · of the great Macedonian conqueror, but there was a problem. Alexander had a battle scar across his forehead. The artist did not want to include this blemish in the portrait. Yet if he omitted it, the picture would not be a true likeness. So he portrayed the emperor as leaning on his elbow with his forefinger on his brow. By this posture the scar on the forehead was completely covered. So it is always with the finger of love. It covers a multitude of sins.

We judge without authority, without knowledge, without love. Finally, judging others blinds us to our own sins. We see the smallest faults of others and are thus blinded to our own greater ones. "Why do you see the speck that is in your brother's eye, but do not notice the log that is in your own

---

* Tournier, Dr. Paul, *Guilt and Grace* (Harper and Brothers), p. 124.

eye?" asks Jesus. "Or how can you say to your brother, 'Let me take the speck out of your eye,' when there is the log in your own eye? You hypocrite, first take the log out of your own eye, and then you will see clearly to take the speck out of your brother's eye" (Matt. 7:3–5). And Helmut Thielicke adds, "If love ever discovers a speck in someone else's eye, it discovers it in order to help remove it gently; it does not discover the speck in order to exult and forget the log in its own eye."

If we must judge, let us judge the only person we have authority to judge, the only person we know anything about— ourselves! Such judgment leads to salvation.

The Pharisee saw the speck in the publican's eye but was blind to the log in his own eye: "God, I thank thee that I am not as other men are. . . ." The publican, on the other hand, didn't look at anybody else; he saw the log in his own eye and prayed that God might remove it: "God, be merciful to me, a sinner." "And," says the Gospel, "He went down to his house justified. . . ."

Chapter Thirty-Five

ONE THING WORSE THAN BLINDNESS

YEARS AGO A PERSON SAID to Helen Keller, who was born blind and deaf, that the worst thing that can happen to a person is to be blind. Quick as a flash Helen Keller replied, "Ah, but there is one thing that *is* worse; that is *to have eyes and not to see.*"

The Gospels tell how Jesus healed two blind men. Not many of us are blind physically as these two men were, but there are many other ways in which we can be blind.

There is the story of the man who was riding in a crowded streetcar. He couldn't bear to be comfortably seated because standing just beside him was a mother holding a small baby in her arms. So what did he do? He closed his eyes so that he would not see her! That made him feel better. How many of us do the same thing as we go through life? All around us there are wounded people—people who are carrying heavy burdens, hurt people, people who are starving for a kind word of love and affection. We see these people and yet like the passenger on the streetcar, we close our eyes to their needs! Then one day we learn that one of these persons has become emotionally ill or has committed suicide. Is there anything worse than blindness? Only one thing: to have eyes and not to see!

Psychologists tell us that *we see what we are looking for.* A famous hunter of tigers who had just returned from India met a Christian missionary who had also recently returned from the same country. The hunter said to the missionary, "I can't see what you missionaries are accomplishing in India. During my stay in India, I didn't see one Christian convert." The missionary then asked the hunter if he had seen any tigers. "Of course," said the hunter, "I saw many tigers. The reason I went to India was to hunt them." Whereupon the missionary said that he had been in India for twenty years but had never seen a tiger. He had been too busy looking for Christians!

We see what we are looking for. The hunter looks for tigers and finds them. The missionary looks for other Christians and finds them. Some people never see God because they have never really looked for Him. They never find Him because they have never really sought Him. ". . . seek after the Lord your God and you will find him if you search after him with all your heart and with all your soul" (Deut. 4:29). The Lord reveals himself to those who look for Him. Those who do not look for Him remain blind to His existence. Is there anything worse than blindness? Only one thing: to have eyes and not to see God.

A person awoke one morning and looked out of his hotel window. The whole town seemed ugly and drab. Even the sunshine seemed too faint to relieve the gloom. He was depressed and saddened. A little while later he walked out of the hotel and instantly the whole picture changed. It was a bright and beautiful day. The air was cool and clear and the town was actually pretty. He realized then where the fault lay. The window in the hotel room was so grimy and dirty that it made everything outside look dull. The fault was not in the day or in the town but in the dirty window.

G. B. Shaw said once, "Better keep yourself clean and bright; you are the window through which you must see the world." How often we look out at other people through windows clouded by prejudice, jealousy and conceit. The result is that we see people not as they are but as they are distorted by our hatred. Heraclitus said once, "Eyes and ears are bad witnesses to those who have barbarian souls." How different it is to look out at other people through windows that have been cleansed by repentance and the love of Christ. Then we see in every person the image of God. Then we see every person not as we think he is but as he really is. Then we look out at the world with hope and with love and with faith. Is there anything worse than blindness? Only one thing: to have eyes and not to see.

Henry Ford once knew a man whose goal in life was to make as much money as possible. One day he brought this man a package. Opening it, he found a pair of eyeglasses but instead of lenses in the frames there were two silver dollars. Mr. Ford asked his friend to put them on. He did. "Now tell me what you see," asked Mr. Ford. "I can't see anything," replied the friend. "These dollars are in the way." "I wanted to teach you," said Mr. Ford, "that if your goal in life is dollars and only dollars, you will be blinded to some of the other values in life that money can never buy."

It is not only by dollars that we are blinded.

Guidepost magazine tells the story of a woman who had cared for her invalid mother for many years. One day the mother died. Following the funeral the brother came to her house and took the family silver tea set which the mother had given to the daughter. The woman was so angry with her brother for taking the set which belonged to her that she refused to speak to him or his family from that time on. Years later she received a telegram that her brother had passed away suddenly of a heart attack. She was still so angry that she considered not attending the funeral, but then she changed her mind and decided to go. At the funeral she saw her sister-in-law and her brother's grown children. She saw her brother in the casket. All of this shocked her into a realization of what she had done. She had allowed a silver tea set to blind her to her brother and his family all these years. She had placed a silver tea set above her love for her brother. Now he was gone and the children were grown and she had missed all those years during which she could have been with them enjoying their friendship. She walked over and kissed her sister-in-law and the children.

As we read the story of Jesus healing the two blind men, we are reminded that we too are often blinded in life. Sometimes we blind ourselves simply by closing our eyes to someone in need. We blind ourselves to God and His will for us simply because we do not look for Him. We look for many other things in life, and we find them; but we do not look for the most important—God. Sometimes we allow our vision of our fellow man to be distorted by prejudice. Often we are blinded by money or even by something like a silver tea set. We blind ourselves to the things that matter most in life. We blind ourselves to the things that make for peace and happiness. We blind ourselves to the whole meaning and purpose of life. How blind we can make ourselves—blind because of the things we can see but do not see. Is there anything worse than blindness? Only one thing: to have eyes and not to see.

If we are to see again, another miracle must take place. We must come to Jesus and ask Him prayerfully and with faith to open our eyes as He opened the eyes of the two blind men. Then we will begin to see. Then we will come to realize that without Jesus no man can truly see and with Him no man can be truly blind. He is the opener of the eyes of the soul. "I am the light of the world. He who follows me shall not walk in darkness but shall have the light of life."

Vance Havner tells of a passenger on a long train trip who was so enthralled by the journey that every few moments he would look at the scenery and say, "Wonderful!" Finally one traveler, overcome by curiosity, asked him, "How is it that while the rest of us are worn out with this monotonous trip, you are having the time of your life and you keep saying, 'Wonderful!' " He answered, "Until a few days ago I was blind. A great doctor has just operated on me and given me my sight. Now, what is ordinary to the rest of you is 'out of the world' to me."

This is the kind of joy we experience when Jesus opens our eyes. We see beauties we never saw before and we make our way through this world praising and glorifying our Lord Jesus.

Chapter Thirty-Six

THE SACRAMENT OF
HOLY COMMUNION

I HEARD SOMEONE TELL the other day how dinner is served down on the farm. All the children and the hired help come in from the fields at noon. They wash their hands and sit at the table. Before the food is served, the mail is read. Then instructions are given as to what chores must be completed that afternoon and evening. After this is finished, the food is served to give everyone the strength to carry out the instructions just received.

Something similar takes place in every liturgy. In the first part of the liturgy—called the Liturgy of the Word—we receive the Word of God. God gives us His instructions as to what He wants us to do, how He wants us to live. We receive these instructions in the Epistle lesson, the Gospel lesson, and the sermon. But we are too weak to carry out the Word of God. We lack strength. That is why in the second part of the liturgy—called the Liturgy of the Faithful—God comes to strengthen us in our weakness. He gives us the power we need. He gives us Himself—the Bread of Life—through the Sacrament of Holy Communion.

What is Holy Communion? How can we best prepare for it?

Dr. Panayiotis Trembelas, professor of theology at the University of Athens, writes that when Christ was born in Bethlehem of Judea, He chose to be born not of a mother who was listed in "Who's Who," but of a poor, humble, pure peasant girl. He chose as His place of entry into this world not a palace but a cold, damp cave that served as a stable for animals. Who would have thought at the time that this child born of this humble mother in such a desolate place was God himself? Yet doesn't this very same thing happen again in the Sacrament of Holy Communion? Doesn't the all-powerful Christ, Lord of heaven and earth, who holds the whole world in His hands, who is worshipped by all creation, doesn't He, even in this Sacrament, shed His divine glory and majesty which would render Him unapproachable, and offer himself to us under the humble forms of bread and wine?

What happened in Bethlehem long ago happens again today whenever the liturgy is celebrated. Christ comes to us again quietly, humbly, disguised under the forms of bread and wine. Have you ever imagined what would happen if Christ were to descend on the altar with the same glorified body with which the disciples saw Him ascending into heaven? Who of us would dare approach Him? Or if He should offer us His body as it was when it was taken down from the cross on Good Friday? Who of us would dare touch it? Through the great Sacrament of Holy Communion the Lord makes himself utterly approachable, disguising himself, even as He did in the manger, and coming to us ever so humbly under the forms of bread and wine. The Sacrament of Communion is the perpetuation of Christmas. In celebrating Christmas we observe not only God's coming into the world thousands of years ago; we celebrate also His coming into the world today to be born in the manger of our soul through this great Sacrament.

When Elijah was fleeing from Jezebel, he lay down under a tree in the wilderness and longed for death. "And he cast himself down and slept in the shadow of the juniper tree and behold an angel of the Lord touched him, and said: arise and eat! He looked, and behold there was at his hand a hearth cake and a vessel of water; and he ate and drank and fell asleep again. And the angel of the Lord came a second time, and touched him and said to him: arise and eat: for thou hast yet a great way to go. And he arose and ate, and walked in the strength of that food forty days and forty nights unto the mount of God, Horeb" (II Kings 19:5–8).

God intervened in the life of Elijah at a time of great crisis, sending him miraculous food and drink and then leading him on a 40-day journey through the desert to the mountain where God spoke to him.

When the Jews were in the wilderness on their way to the Promised Land and were in danger of perishing from hunger, the Lord provided them with bread from heaven—manna.

Each morning they would find the bread in the fields and they would gather a day's supply at a time. Thereafter they were never hungry again. Whenever the harvests failed, they still had their manna from heaven to sustain them.

Just as God intervened in the life of Elijah and the Jewish people in the wilderness sending miraculous food to sustain them, so He provides food from heaven today to sustain us in our journey through life.

We read in the 6th chapter of the Gospel according to St. John: "Your fathers ate the manna in the wilderness and they died. This is the bread which comes down from heaven, that a man may eat of it and not die. I am the living bread which came down from heaven; if any one eats of this bread, he will live for ever; and the bread which I shall give for the life of the world is my flesh.

"The Jews disputed among themselves, saying, 'How can this man give us his flesh to eat?' So Jesus said to them, 'Truly, truly, I say to you, unless you eat the flesh of the Son of man and drink his blood, you have no life in you; he who eats my flesh and drinks my blood has eternal life, and I will raise him up at the last day. For my flesh is food indeed, and my blood is drink indeed. He who eats my flesh and drinks my blood abides in me and I in him' " (John 6:49–56).

A Prefigurement

One of the plagues by which Moses sought to impress upon the Pharaoh that it was God's will that he should allow the Jewish people to leave Egypt, was that all the firstborn children of Egypt would be slain on a certain night. To the Jewish people, however, a means of deliverance was provided. Each family head was ordered to slaughter a male lamb, sprinkle its blood on the doorpost and confidently remain in his dwelling. *"And when I see the blood,"* said the Lord, *"I will pass over you, and the plague shall not be upon you to destroy you, when I smite the land of Egypt."*

This event was a preview of what was to happen thousands of years later when the Lamb of God, Jesus, saved us by shedding His precious blood on the cross. Just as the blood of lambs saved the Jewish people from the sword of the destroying angel, even more so does the blood of the Lamb of God save us today from sin and eternal damnation. God continues to offer us His saving blood through the Sacrament of Holy Communion. He offers it to us for the forgiveness of sins and unto life eternal.

The Horizontal Dimension of the Eucharist

Most of us are aware of the *vertical dimension* of the Eucharist, of the fact that it unites us to God as His people: "He who eats my flesh and drinks my blood abides in me and I in him," said Jesus. It is this Sacrament which makes it possible for us to say with St. Paul, "Christ liveth in me." And through this Sacrament, we can leave the Lord's table with the glowing courage of the same St. Paul who said, "I can do all things through Christ who strengthens me."

Few Christians, however, realize the *horizontal dimension* of the Eucharist, the fact that it unites us not only to God, but also to each other. Through the Eucharist we all become one in Christ since the same Christ comes to dwell in all of us. The Fathers of the Church take for granted the unity of the individual to God through the Eucharist. What they stress and emphasize greatly is the horizontal dimension of Communion— our becoming one with each other in Christ. "The very fact that we all share one bread makes us one body," says St. Paul.

Christ tells us that the first and greatest commandment is love of God *and man.* Yet we all know from experience that it is not always easy to love our fellow man. God knew that this was a difficult commandment. That is why He gave us the Sacrament of Communion through which He gives us His own strength to enable us to practice this commandment of love.

The Orthodox Church emphasizes love more than anything else. Dr. Otto Nall, Bishop of the Methodist Church in Minnesota, wrote, "Orthodoxy stresses love . . . if Roman Catholic Christianity is the religion of the 'law,' and Protestant Christianity is the religion of 'faith,' then Orthodox Christianity is the religion of love. That shines through all its life."

If Orthodox Christianity is the religion of love, it is so

because it believes not only that all men are created in the image of God, and that Christ died for all and that all are called to the resurrection in the new life, but Orthodoxy is the religion of love especially because it believes that through the Eucharist Christ comes to live in us thus making us all a community of brothers and sisters. This is why the liturgy in our church is never celebrated in private, just by the priest alone, but always with the family of God—the congregation—present. This is done in order to express the horizontal dimension of the Eucharist, i.e., the fact that by receiving the Body and Blood of Christ we are all joined together in one body, one family—the family of God.

This means that the same Christ who comes to us in Holy Communion comes to us also in the person of our neighbor, our fellow parishioner, our fellow Christian: Christ lives in every person I meet. "Forasmuch as you did it unto one of these the least of my brethren you did it to me," said Jesus. The way I treat my fellow man is the way I treat Christ. To honor Christ in the Sacrament of Communion and to dishonor Him in the person of my fellow man is sacrilege, sin, hypocrisy. As St. John Chrysostom writes, "Do you wish to honor the Body of Christ? Then do not look down or disdain Him when you see Him in rags. After having honored Him in church with silken vestments do not leave Him to die of cold outside for lack of clothing. For it is the same Jesus who says 'This is my Body' and who says 'You saw me hungry and did not give me to eat—What you have refused to the least of these my little ones, you have refused it to me!' "

The same Christ, then, who comes to us in the Eucharist comes to us also in the people we meet and with whom we live. The Lord Jesus tells us specifically that we are not to approach the altar to receive His body unless we have first established a relationship of love and forgiveness with all our fellow men on the horizontal level. *"If you are offering your gift at the altar, and there remember that your brother has something against you, leave your gift there before the altar and go: first be reconciled to your brother, and then come and offer your gift"* (Matt. 5:23, 24).

When Are We in Condition to Receive?

Fulton Oursler tells about an incident in his childhood when his mother, after dressing him in his Sunday best, warned him not to get off the front steps. "We'll be walking over to see your aunt," she promised, "and I want you to be neat."

He waited obediently until the baker's son came along and called him a sissy. Soon they got into a fight and the next thing Fulton knew he was sitting in the middle of a mud puddle. With a twinge of conscience he returned to the front steps.

Presently, down the street came the ice-cream peddler, pushing his cart. Forgetting his disobedience, Fulton ran indoors and begged his mother for a penny.

"Just look at yourself!" she exclaimed. "You're in no condition to ask for anything."

There are many persons who feel the same way about receiving Communion. How often we hear people say, "I'm in no condition to receive Communion." When is a person "in condition" to receive Communion?

Have you ever had the feeling on a particular occasion that you shouldn't take Communion? Many of us have that feeling occasionally. We feel unworthy; we feel that it would be hypocritical to take Communion at that time; we feel that we aren't "good enough" to participate. I think this is a good feeling to have before Communion. No Christian should ever come to Communion with the feeling that he deserves to come because he is "good enough." If anyone has this feeling, he should not come. For this is a good sign that he is not good enough; that his soul has been poisoned by the sin of pride.

There is one thing we should always remember about Communion. And that is this: When the Lord Jesus invites us to Communion, He is calling us *not* to PERFECTION but to CONFESSION. If we are not "good enough"—as none of us is—then let us repent and come to confession to receive the Lord's forgiveness, to let Him cleanse us, to let Him make us worthy. "Him that cometh to me I will in no wise cast out," said Jesus.

We Come to Take and Give

We come to this Sacrament not only to TAKE Communion but also to GIVE ourselves in communion with Christ to God the Father. In the Eucharist we are joined with the Lord Jesus in His offering, in His sacrifice. We are able to be joined with Him because He is the Head of the Body of which we, by baptism, have been made members. Together with the whole church, living and departed, we are united with Christ in His sacrifice, and with it we put our gifts, our prayers and our sufferings, to be offered by Christ to His Father. We are not only *at* the altar, we are *on* the altar. The bread and wine which the priest places on God's altar represent us. When the priest offers the bread and the wine to God, we kneel. We remember that these are our gifts the priest is offering to God: our love, our thanksgiving, our obedience. We remember that we are *on* the altar offering ourselves to God with Christ under the forms of bread and wine.

The sacrament of the Eucharist is given to us not primarily that we may do something but that we may be *someone,* that each of us, upon receiving the body and blood of Christ, may go out and be another CHRIST in the world today, that we may be possessed with a divine restlessness about the situation of the world, that we may go out and plunge ourselves into the midst of the world's problems and bring to them Christ's answer, Christ's solution, Christ's love, Christ's understanding, Christ's peace, Christ's hope.

Bishop Fulton Sheen writes, "There are three intimacies in life: hearing, seeing, touching. Our first contact with anyone who loves us is to *hear* his voice, our second is to *see* him, the third (and this is reserved only for intimates) is the privilege of *touch*. We *hear* Christ in the Scriptures, we *see* Him by the eyes of faith, but we *touch* Him in the Eucharist." To be "in condition" to "touch Him," the Lord requires not perfection but repentance, confession and a new life in Christ Jesus.

"Come now, let us reason together, says the Lord: though your sins be like scarlet, they shall be as white as snow; though

they are red like crimson, they shall become like wool" (Isa.
1:18).

"The Lord is merciful and gracious,
Slow to anger and abounding in steadfast love. . . .
He does not deal with us according to our sins,
Nor requite us according to our iniquities.
For as the heavens are high above the earth,
So great is his love toward those who fear him;
As far as the east is from the west,
So far does he remove our transgressions from us.
As a father pities his children,
So the Lord pities those who fear him.
For he knows our frame;
He remembers that we are dust."

Psalm 103:8–14

Chapter Thirty-Seven

THE MEANING OF THE CROSS

WHEN GOD MADE THE OYSTER, He guaranteed him absolute economic and social security. He built the oyster a shell to protect him from his enemies. When hungry, the oyster simply opens his shell, and food rushes in for him.

But when God made the eagle, He said, "The blue sky is the limit. Go and build your own house," and the eagle builds his nest on the highest mountain crag, where storms threaten him every day. For food he flies through miles and miles of rain and snow and wind.

It is interesting that the eagle, not the oyster, is the symbol of America.

It is interesting also that the symbol of Christianity is not a cream puff or a rocking chair but a cross—a cross with a man hanging on it; a man who is God in human flesh, who challenges us: "If any man will come after me, let him deny himself and take up his cross and follow me."

On September 14 of each year Orthodox Christians observe a great feast day dedicated to the cross: the Feast of the Raising of the Precious Cross. Let us consider this feast day as it speaks about the cross and its meaning to us.

The cross appears on almost everything used in God's services: altars, linens, churches, books, vestments. During the liturgy we make the sign of the cross countless times. In our personal devotions we make it morning and evening, before and after all our prayers, in temptation, in bodily dangers, before every important action or undertaking.

St. Cyril of Jerusalem wrote in the 4th century: "Let us then not be ashamed to confess the Crucified. Be the cross our seal, made with boldness by our fingers on our brow and in everything; over the bread we eat and the cups we drink, in our comings in and in our goings out; before our sleep, when

we lie down and when we awake; when we are traveling and
when we are at rest."

I wonder if we have ever pondered how rich in meaning is
the sign of the cross as we Orthodox Christians make it.

To make the sign of the cross we join the thumb, the index
and the middle finger of the right hand at their tips, and at the
same time we rest the fourth and little finger in the palm of
the hand. First we touch the forehead, then the breast and immediately following the right and left shoulder in that order.
At the end we let the hand fall to the side as we make a bow.
The thumb, the index and middle finger touching each other
at their tips represent the Holy Trinity: God the Father who
created us, God the Son who saved us, and God the Holy Spirit
who abides in us: three persons in one God—the Holy Trinity.
Then we let the fourth and little fingers representing the two
natures of Jesus—human and divine—drop into the palm of
the hand to denote that Jesus *"came down from heaven"* and
became man for our salvation. Thus, we make the sign of the
cross to remind ourselves of who God is and what He did for
us. Every time we cross ourselves we recall the great price He
paid to redeem us.

But through the sign of the cross we express also *our response* to the sacrifice of Christ: we place our hand to the forehead and promise that with God's help we shall endeavor to
know Him with all our mind; we place our hand to our breast
promising that our purpose in life will be to *love* God with all
our heart; then we place our hand to the right and left shoulders
promising to *serve* God with all our strength. Thus we give expression to the greatest Christian commandment: "Thou shalt
love the Lord thy God with all thy mind, and with all thy heart,
and with all thy strength, and with all thy soul." Finally we
bow to acknowledge that we and all men are under God's dom-
ination and rule. The sign of the cross, then, as we Orthodox
Christians make it expresses some of the most basic and funda-
mental teachings of our Orthodox faith: the Trinity, the Incarnation, the greatest Christian commandment, and commitment
to Christ. It is the body praying together with the soul. The
whole man prays to God.

To the people of Christ's day the cross was the greatest symbol of shame. It was to them what the electric chair or the hangman's noose would be for us today. Crucifixion was a method of execution reserved only for slaves and the lowest criminals. It was unthinkable for a Roman citizen to be executed by crucifixion. It was that kind of death, the most dreaded in the ancient world, the death of slaves and criminals, that Jesus died. Yet Jesus took the greatest "minus" sign in the ancient world, the cross, and transformed it into a great "plus" sign. So we today, because of Christ, can take all the great minus signs of life—sin, death, suffering, pain—and transform them into plus signs. Death, for example, was a great minus sign in life until Christ, by His resurrection, transformed it into the plus sign of life eternal. Sin was another minus sign in life until Christ, by His forgiving love, transformed it into the plus sign of reconciliation with God. The crucifixion and resurrection of Christ have added a great plus sign to life.

The cross of Christ shows us also the severity of sin. Sin is not just breaking a divine commandment; it is that, but it is more than that. When we look at the cross and Him who hangs there, we see sin for what it really is: the crucifixion of God, the breaking not of a commandment but of the heart of God.

The cross of Christ reveals also the worth of man in the eyes of God. What is a man worth? We shall never know the answer to this question until we look at Christ—the Son of man and the Son of God—hanging on the cross. Then we know that man has value and worth and dignity not only because he is created in the image of God but also because God gives His only begotten Son to redeem him. This is the price tag God places on man. He is worth as much as the precious blood of His Son.

The cross enables us also to look in on the heart of God. When we look to Moses and the Ten Commandments in the Old Testament we learn of the stern justice of God. His universe is law-abiding. But when we look away from Mt. Sinai to the cross on Mt. Calvary we know that God is far more than law and justice. He is love and mercy. The cross becomes a window through which we can look into the heart of God.

Leslie Weatherhead tells of a traveller being aboard a ship one dark night in the Mediterranean. They were passing Stromboli, the famous volcano. Suddenly the volcano became active. There was a great burst of flame lighting up the ocean for miles around. An awe-inspiring flash filled the horizon. Then, in a little while, it was dark again. It occurred to the viewer that Stromboli tells of what is always happening in the center of the earth. The great fires and molten rock surge and churn constantly. Only occasionally does the force that is there find a fault line and burst out as at Stromboli.

It is the same with the cross. It allows us to catch only a glimpse of the infinite love for man that has always burned in the heart of God.

A father managed to get his son out of trouble again and again until finally he felt forced to give up on the boy. "I have had to wash my hands of him," he said. "What else could I do?" Well, whatever the complete opposite of "washing our hands" of one is, God did it on the cross. The cross is eternal proof that God loves us, that He is after us, that we matter to Him, that He will not hesitate ever to give "his only-begotten Son that whoever believes in him may not perish but have life everlasting."

The finest response to the love of Christ on the cross is to pick up the cross and carry it after Christ, matching action to His challenge when He says, "If any man would come after me, let him deny himself and take up his cross and follow me."

Look at some of those who through the centuries took up the cross and followed Jesus.

Simon of Cyrene—the man who was compelled to carry the cross to Calvary when Jesus collapsed under its weight.

Peter, James and John—beaten for preaching the Gospel in the market place against orders.

Paul—jailed, persecuted, slandered, finally killed—carrying his cross.

The early Christian martyrs—singing in the Roman arena as the lions came at them, lighting up Roman festivals as human torches—carrying their crosses.

A young person today who, in the face of tremendous pressure from his friends to do as the crowd does, chooses Christ instead of the crowd—carrying his cross.

These are crucified Christians who use the cross not only

as an external adornment or as a symbol on their altars but also keep it enshrined in their lives, who lift it high for all to look through and see the infinite love for man that burns eternally in the heart of God.

The Feast of the Raising of the Precious Cross commemorates the discovery of the precious cross. The cross, as you may recall, remained lost for nearly four hundred years. It was discovered in the fourth century by St. Helen, Constantine's mother. St. John Chrysostom, in 395, speaks of the three crosses discovered by the Empress Helen beneath the mound of Golgotha: that of Christ was identified because it was found in the middle and bore the inscription.

A certain legend states that the Empress Helen did not know where on Golgotha to look for the cross. As she searched she came upon a sweet-smelling plant and decided to dig under the spot. It was there that she found the cross. From that time on, according to tradition, the plant was named Basilikos in Greek, Basil in English, which means literally, royal, regal or "the plant of the King." Basil is often used in the religious services of the Eastern Orthodox Church. We use it, for example, for the sprinkling of holy water during religious ceremonies. It has taken the place of another plant, hyssop, which was used in the religious ceremonies in the Old Testament.

To celebrate the discovery of the precious cross the bishop, standing on a platform in the Church of the Resurrection in Jerusalem, raised the cross as the faithful sang "Kyrie eleison." This ceremony of the "ipsosis," or raising, was celebrated in the early church since the fourth century to commemorate the discovery and raising of the cross out of the mound on Golgotha where it lay hidden for nearly 400 years.

St. Cyril of Jerusalem, in 349, said, "Already the whole universe is filled with fragments of the wood of the cross." There is an interesting custom that we still practice today that dates back to this time. Most Christians at this time carried with them pieces of wood which they believed were parts of the original cross. When danger threatened, they would touch the wood, thereby signifying that by the power of God through the cross they would be able to endure. This is how the habit of "knocking on wood" to avoid danger originated. Originally it was not "knocking" on wood but touching a piece of wood which they believed to be a fragment of the cross.

In the year 628 A.D. the infidel Persians succeeded in pushing back the Byzantine armies. They captured Jerusalem, then belonging to the Christian empire. Among the booty they carried off was the very cross upon which our Lord Jesus Christ had been crucified.

The Christian Empire could not tolerate such irreverence and desecration. Fresh forces were organized to recapture Jerusalem and win back the precious cross from the pagan enemies.

Under Emperor Heraclius III the Persians were repulsed and the precious cross was recovered. The victory was celebrated in a most fitting manner. The ceremony of the Raising of the Precious Cross was again performed amid great rejoicing; this time to celebrate not only its *discovery* by St. Helen, but also its *recovery* from the hands of the infidel. The chanting of the "Kyrie eleison" (Lord, have mercy) arose in unison as the cross was raised once again before the adoring eyes of thousands of Christians.

This centuries-old ceremony is repeated every year on the Feast of the Precious Cross. The precious cross of Christ, surrounded by sweet-smelling basil, is first lowered to the ground, to denote that for 400 years it was buried, lost, and then it is raised to commemorate its discovery by St. Helen in the fourth century and its eventual recovery from the Persians in the seventh century.

But there is a deeper significance to the raising of the cross as we practice it on this day. Our Lord refers to it when He says in John 3:14, 15, ". . . as Moses lifted up the serpent in the wilderness, so must the Son of man be lifted up, that whoever believes in him may have eternal life." Jesus is referring to the time when the Israelites were in the wilderness. They were rebellious and complaining. Because of their disobedience, God sent poisonous snakes to punish them. The people were dying from the bites. They went to Moses with a protest and an appeal for help. Moses, as always, took his troubles to God. God told him to raise a standard of a brazen serpent and to tell the people to look at it when bitten. Healing would come by looking at the standard. And it did. Those who looked at the brazen serpent were healed. Perhaps this is why the serpent today is used as an emblem by medical doctors.

As Moses lifted the serpent in the wilderness, says Jesus, so must the Son of man be lifted upon the cross that whoever believes in Him might have eternal life. Thus, every year on this Feast, the Church raises the cross in our midst. She raises it so that we today may find healing and strength in the up-lifted cross of Christ. For we, too, become infected with the deadly poison of sin and guilt. Salvation for us, too, is in a look—a look of faith and repentance and commitment to the crucified and risen Christ.

I close with the following words of Archbishop William Temple taken from his book *The Faith and Modern Thought*— words that show how God speaks to us through the cross. He writes:

"When Reason says, 'It is God who made all the world: He is therefore responsible; it is He who should suffer,' we answer, 'Yes, of course; He does suffer; look at the cross!' And when Reason cries, 'If God were the loving God of whom you speak, He could not endure the misery of His children, His heart would break'; we answer, 'Yes, of course; it does break; look at the cross!' And when Reason exclaims, 'God is infinite and ineffable; it is blasphemy to say we know Him; we cannot know Him'; we answer, 'No, not perfectly; but enough to love Him; look at the cross!' " *

---

* Temple, William, *The Faith and Modern Thought* (London: Macmillan and Co., 1910), p. 168.

Chapter Thirty-Eight

WHAT ARE YOU WEARING?

In an issue of the *Reader's Digest* there appeared an article entitled "Come As You Are." The author of the article said in part:

"On motor trips with my family, we see this sign in front of more and more roadside restaurants: 'Come as you are.'

"And darned if people don't do just that—by the millions!

"They crawl out of their cars almost as nature made them. . . . They come in short shorts . . . in stretch pants, in Capri pants, in T-shirts, in undershirts. . . . They come as they are to the laundromat, to the movie theatre. . . .

"Business places have had to give in. Restaurants that used to have signs reading 'Gentlemen will wear ties' (and in some cases supplied them) have settled for signs saying 'Gentlemen will wear trousers.'

"The real low in come-as-you-are-ness is a woman in hair curlers. These should be worn only in the bedroom with the door locked; but no, women wear them to the post office and to the supermarket."

There are now even "COME AS YOU ARE" parties. In case you haven't heard, the host at such a party does not send invitations. He calls his guests on the phone and tells them to come right away. They mustn't stop to change their clothes. They simply drop whatever they're doing and go.

The result, as you can imagine, is often very humorous. Ladies come in housecoats, or with curlers in their hair. A man who has been painting may show up with paint splattered all over his face. If someone takes time to clean up or dress up, he spoils the fun. The fun is to see what people look like when they're relaxing or working at home. So the rule is "Come as you are."

Jesus once told a parable of a man who came to a wedding

feast just as he was. In Matthew 22:11–14 Jesus tells of a king who came in to look at the guests whom he had invited to a wedding feast. He saw there a man who had no wedding garment. Here we need to understand that in those days the person (the host) who invited guests to a marriage feast, provided each guest with a special wedding garment. This was to be worn upon entrance to the banquet hall. Upon seeing this person who had no wedding garment, the king said to him, "Friend, how did you get in here without a wedding garment?" The guest was speechless. Then the king said to the attendants, "Bind him hand and foot, and cast him into the outer darkness." The guest "came as he was" and he was not accepted.

There is another marriage feast to which the King, God, invites all of us. It is the great banquet of the Last Supper: the Sacrament of Holy Communion. This is a real wedding feast because through this Sacrament the Lord Jesus actually weds himself to us and we to Him in the most intimate relationship that exists between God and man: "He who eats my flesh and drinks my blood abides in me and I in him" (John 6:56).

The parable tells us that there was one man who had not taken the trouble to come properly prepared. Could it be so with some of us? We approach the Sacrament without having truly repented. Our sins may be hidden from human view. Our fellow parishioners may not suspect us. But there is One who knows, One whom we cannot escape. It is a terrible moment when He says to us, "Friend, how did you get in here without a wedding garment?"

What is the proper wedding garment? How does one obtain it?

The same God who invites us to the marriage feast, also provides a wedding garment for all who would come. Man does not buy or earn this wedding garment; it is given to him by God. It is the gift of God. It is the white robe of salvation in Christ. St. Paul speaks of this garment when he says, "For as many of you as were baptized into Christ have put on Christ" (Gal. 3:27). At baptism we are cleansed of sin. We are made pure. But we also put on Christ as we put on a new suit or dress. Yet it is not only at baptism that we put on Christ; if we are true Christians, we are to put Him on every day. Ev-

ery day we are to put on "the mind of Christ" (I Cor. 2:16)
so that we think what He thinks, see what He sees, will what
He wills. Every day we are to put on His compassion, His
kindness, His lowliness, His meekness, His patience, His forgiveness and above all His love, which binds everything together in perfect harmony (Col. 3:12–14).

Yet when many of us come to the great banquet of God's
presence, the Sacrament of Communion, we come as we are.
We come with little or no sorrow for our sins. We come with
little or no determination to overcome and forsake our sins.
We come feeling that God will forgive us anyway; it's His
business to forgive just as it's a baker's business to bake bread.
We come and then we go back to the same old sins we were
committing before. We take God's love and justice lightly. We
come without real repentance. We come trusting in our own
goodness, feeling that we have done so many good works that
even God himself is indebted to us. He must accept us. We
come wearing the garment of our own self-righteousness
and pride. This is exactly the garment the king does not recog-
nize as His own. "He saw there a man who had no wedding
garment. And he said to him, 'Friend, how did you get in
here without a wedding garment?' " The guest was speechless.

When God invites us to the wedding feast He does not say,
"Come as you are." He says, "Come better than you are. Come
clothed with Christ." When the priest invites us to partake of
the Eucharist during the liturgy, he faces the congregation
with the chalice and says not "Come as you are," but "Come,
with the fear of God, with faith and with love." Come, but
before you come, make sure you destroy the old sinful man
within you. Make sure you have repented of your sins and
confessed them. Make sure you detest them, and have decided
to forsake them. Come, but before you come take off the masks
of hypocrisy. "Put to death . . . what is earthly in you: immorality, impurity, passion, evil desire . . . covetousness . . . anger,
malice, slander . . . foul talk" (Col 3:5–9). Come, but before
you come make sure you put on the wedding garment of the
King: put on Christ. Come clothed with repentance and forgiveness and love and humility.

God said to Moses at the burning bush, "Do not come near.

Put off your shoes from your feet, for the place on which you are standing is holy ground" (Ex. 3:5).

God asked him to remove the habitual shoes with which he walked around every day, for he was now standing on holy ground. Should it be any different for us when we stand on the holy ground of His presence in the great Sacrament of Communion?

When we come into the presence of God, we don't wear casual clothes as if it didn't matter much. This is why the Orthodox priest does not wear his everyday street clothes when he celebrates the divine liturgy. He wears special clothes called vestments to denote that we are to come into the presence of God not as we are but better than we are, clothed with Christ, His love, forgiveness and humility.

Man today experiences a deep nakedness; it is nakedness of the soul: a soul that has lost God. Man has tried to be his own God and has thus come to discover his weakness and insecurity. Look, for example, how naked men feel in regard to the H-bomb. How naked they feel in the presence of disease, illness and death. This is perhaps why, when a man finds salvation (Christ), he speaks of being "clothed" with it. Emil Brunner, the theologian, says, "We must . . . wrap ourselves up in the grace of God in Jesus Christ just as a little child, when it becomes afraid, wraps itself up in the apron of its mother, has a good cry there, and is . . . so comforted that it jumps again happily in the street."

Perhaps our great need today is to wrap ourselves up in the grace of God regularly through prayer, through the Bible and through the Sacrament of Communion. The person who daily wraps himself up in the grace of God covers the nakedness of his soul and is "clothed" with a security that fears neither H-bomb nor death. In the words of the Apostle Paul, "Who shall separate us from the love of Christ? Shall tribulation, or distress, or persecution, or famine, or nakedness, or peril, or sword? . . . No, in all these things we are more than conquerors through him who loved us" (Rom. 8:35–37).

PRAYER

"Into the glorious company of Thy saints how shall I enter, Lord; I who am so unworthy. For should I, too, dare to enter the wedding chamber my robe betrays me, for it is not a wedding garment and I shall be bound and cast out by the angels. Cleanse my soul, O Lord, from wickedness, and of Thy compassion save me."

—Prayer from the Orthodox Service of
Preparation for Holy Communion

Chapter Thirty-Nine

REPENT, FOR THE KINGDOM OF GOD IS AT HAND

ONE DAY ST. AMBROSE, ARCHBISHOP OF MILAN, refused to give the Sacrament of Communion to Emperor Theodosius because the latter had ordered the population of Thessalonica to be massacred. The emperor protested, "Why should I be rejected," he asked, "when David who was both murderer and an adulterer was not rejected by God?" St. Ambrose turned to Emperor Theodosius and said, "You have imitated David in his crime; now imitate him in his repentance."

The first sermon Jesus ever preached was not long; it was very short, only one sentence long: "Repent, for the kingdom of God is at hand." It is said that the whole Gospel of Jesus can be summed up in this one word: REPENT!

What is repentance? Robert Frost called it a "one-man revolution." It is just that: a revolution not against the world or other people but against the evil in oneself.

When we do something we know is sinful we lose our self-respect. We have difficulty living with ourselves. We cannot stand the guilt, the pangs of conscience, the sleepless nights. There are two things we can do with these guilt feelings. We can try to push them out of mind, or forget them since to remember them causes us such great pain. We call this repression. But repression doesn't work. Repressed guilt feelings are one of the greatest causes of mental illness. The alternative to repression is repentance which means that one is honest before God. Instead of trying to repress or hide his sin, one admits it to God in confession and seeks His forgiveness. God not only forgives but also accepts the penitent. As a result the former sinner is better able to accept himself and live with himself.

Repentance requires a *CHANGED MIND*. In fact, the Greek word for repentance *metanoia* means just that: a changed mind. It means that one comes to see the wrongness of the whole attitude of mind which made him act as he did. We experience a changed mind as a result of looking at our Model, Christ. Everybody who is confronted with Christ knows that he needs cleansing. "Depart from me, Lord," said Peter when Jesus approached him, "for I am a sinful man." The first thing necessary for repentance is the vision of God in Christ.

The second thing involved in true repentance is a *CHANGED HEART*. A changed heart is one that experiences true sorrow for its sins. Sorrow is more than regret. A certain youth embezzled his employer's money. His employer found out. The prosecution was about to begin. The boy's pastor pleaded with the employer to be merciful. This would break the heart of the boy's good parents. The money—he promised— would be returned. The employer relented. The prosecution was called off. When the pastor informed the young boy about this, he smiled and seemed to think it was a pity the money had to be paid back. He wasn't sorry for his sins at all. He was only sorry for the price he thought he had to pay. True repentance means I am sorry not because I have been apprehended in my crime but because I have offended God. As David said in his great penitential psalm: "Against thee, thee only, have I sinned."

The third factor involved in true repentance is a *CHANGED DIRECTION*. The change of mind and heart in repentance is so thorough that it leads to a changed direction of life. The Jewish word for repentance means "to turn." This is exactly what true repentance is: a turning away from evil and a turning towards God. One day a man who was lost asked someone how far it was to the city he sought. The man replied, "If you keep going the way you are going, it is about 25,000 miles. But, if you turn back and go this way, it is only about three miles." A U-turn may not be allowed on our streets because it can tie up traffic and cause accidents, but it is often the best thing we can do in life especially when we are headed in the wrong direction. St. Paul made a "U-turn" on the Damascus Road. If repentance is anything, it is a U-turn, a reversing of the direction of life so that we face God. Because we have taken one step down a wrong road is no reason why we should take two.

When we hear the word repentance we immediately think of sinners we know who ought to repent. In other words, we think of someone else. But Jesus does not address the command to repent to someone else. He addresses it to us. If only we would look to ourselves instead of constantly blaming others; if only we would change the direction of our lives instead of waiting for others to do so, we would be far better Christians and this would be a far better world.

Someone said once, "Every time history repeats itself it does so at a higher price." But history does not have to repeat itself if we repent and turn the direction of our life toward God.

A changed mind, a changed heart, and a changed direction lead to a *CHANGED LIFE*. "Bear fruit that befits repentance," said Jesus. It is not enough merely to repent and confess our sins. We must now express our repentance with a new life. "A good tree brings forth good fruit," said Jesus. Repentance takes place inside a man, but it can be seen on the outside. Ugly words are replaced by kind ones, dishonesty by honesty, pride by humility, hatred by love.

A changed life will lead to a *CHANGED SERVICE*. When the Lord asked Peter three times, "Do you love me?" He deepened Peter's repentance for the three times he had denied Him. But at the same time as the Lord deepened Peter's repentance, He called him again to service. "Feed my lambs," He told Peter. True repentance means that we cease serving sin, self and idols, and we turn to the worship and service of the one, true God.

Repentance, then, is truly a "one-man revolution" involving a changed mind, a changed heart, a changed direction, a changed life and a changed service.

Listen to what the great St. John Chrysostom has to say of repentance:

"No sin is so great that it can conquer the munificence of the Master. Even if one is a fornicator, or an adulterer . . . the power of the gift and the love of the Master are great enough to make all these sins disappear and to make the sinner shine more brightly than the rays of the sun . . . .

"And Christ Himself, addressing the whole human race,

said: 'Come to me, all you who labor and are burdened, and I will give you rest . . . . '

"His invitation is one of kindness, His goodness is beyond description . . . . And see whom He calls! Those who have spent their strength in breaking the law, those who are burdened with their sins, those who can no longer lift up their heads, those who are filled with shame, those who can no longer speak out. And why does He call them? Not to demand an accounting, nor to hold court. But why? To relieve them of their pain, to take away their heavy burden. For what could ever be a heavier burden than sin? . . . . 'I shall refresh you who are weighted down by sin,' He says, 'and you who are bent down as if under a burden; I shall grant you remission of your sins. Only come to me!' "

The penitent thief, who was crucified next to Him came. He came to Jesus with repentance, "Lord, remember me when you come into your kingdom." And Jesus said, "Today you will be in paradise with me." He was a thief! He had stolen horses, jewels, money. But now he steals heaven. He picks the lock of the gate of heaven with the key of repentance.

"Repent," said Jesus, "for the kingdom of God is at hand." What is the kingdom of God? It is nothing more than a state in which God is the king and rules. God invaded the world at Christmas. He came to forgive, to enlighten, to lead, to make all things new. He came to reign not on some earthly throne but on the throne of your heart and mine. Those who trust Jesus enough to repent, to make a complete right-about-face from sin and self to God will find, as Jesus said, that "the kingdom of God is within you" (Luke 17:21).